Wading In the Deep End

Difficulties In Scripture & Theology

Travis W. Rogers

Copyright © 2011 Travis W. Rogers

All rights reserved. No portion of this book may be reproduced, stored in a retrieval system, or transmitted in any form or by any means – electronic, mechanical, photocopy, recording, scanning, or other – except for brief quotations in critical reviews or articles, without the prior written permission of the publisher.

Scripture taken (unless otherwise noted) from the NEW AMERICAN STANDARD BIBLE®, Copyright © 1960, 1962, 1963, 1968, 1971, 1972, 1973, 1975, 1977, 1995 by The Lockman Foundation. Used by permission. www.Lockman.org

Scripture notations marked NIV are from the HOLY BIBLE, NEW INTERNATIONAL VERSION®. NIV®. Copyright © 1973, 1978, 1984 by International Bible Society. Used by permission. All rights reserved worldwide.

Scripture notations marked KJV are taken from the Holy Bible, King James Version.

ISBN-10: 1467940992
ISBN-13: 978-1467940993

DEDICATION

To my dear friend Paul Cassidy. You are everything a pastor should be, everything a student needs, and everything a friend could want. Your faithful teaching all those years is the direct reason I have fallen in love with Scripture and has spurred in me a passion to teach others.

CONTENTS

	Acknowledgments	i
	Introduction	ii
1	Apostles and Prophets	1
2	Could Jesus Sin?	6
3	Rules To Live By	11
4	Legalism vs. License	21
5	Does God Hate the Sin or the Sinner?	30
6	Predestination	41
7	Gifts of the Spirit	53
8	Gifts To Edify	73
9	Jesus In Hell	81
10	Gender Neutral?	92
11	Love Someone Into Hell	103
12	Good Works	107
13	Where Does Faith Come From?	112
14	Three Simple Words	119
15	One Way Street	125
16	A Reason To Celebrate	133
17	Choose Responsibly	149

ACKNOWLEDGMENTS

Many thanks to all who graciously contributed to the completion of this book whether it was though casual discussion which prompted chapter ideas or direct critique of said chapters. The result is what you hold in your hands today. I would like to give a special thanks to my pastor, Dr. Alan Thompson, and my friend, Timothy Hulbert, in their careful critiques and plethora of comments. Without them, I am afraid what kind of a mess I would have left you all with. God bless!

INTRODUCTION

From time to time, everybody has questions about Scripture and theology. Whether it be something as simple as what Jesus died for or something as complex as some of the issues addressed in this book, we all have questions. My goal in the book is to answer some of those questions and word them in a way that anyone can understand. The Holy Spirit resides in us (as Christians) and teaches us the deeper things of God. Thankfully, God has also provided the office of teachers to help others understand these deep issues. By the Authority of Scripture, I pray this book will clarify the questions you, as the reader, may have that you may graduate from milk to meat.

Travis W. Rogers

1 APOSTLES AND PROPHETS

There is much debate in the Church as to whether or not apostles and prophets exist in this day and age. Depending on who you ask, the answer will differ. One religious leader may say apostles exist while another may say only prophets exist. Even more, another may claim both are very active in the Church today. Let's see what the Bible has to say on the matter.

Ephesians 2:19-20

> So then you are no longer strangers and aliens, but you are fellow citizens with the saints, and are of God's household, having been built on the foundation of the apostles and prophets, Christ Jesus Himself being the corner stone,

What does this say exactly? Does it say there are no apostles? Does it say there are no prophets? Does it say there are both?

Apostles

Rest assured, there are no apostles in this day and age. Every person in the Bible with the title of apostle was given it by Jesus himself. What do we know of apostles?

1) They were called by Jesus Christ and God the Father (Gal 1:1)
2) They had seen Jesus personally (1 Cor 9:1)
3) The fruits of apostleship would be shown (1 Cor 9:2)
4) They performed signs, wonders, and miracles (2 Cor 12:12)
5) Existed to teach the elect (1 Pet 1:1)
6) Ministered to both Jews and Gentiles (Gal 2:8)

I don't know about you but I am doubtful Christ has returned. If that were the case, the Bible would be a lie since I am still here writing this. Rest assured, the Second Coming has not yet occurred. To claim the title of apostle, one must also be able to claim every one of the items in the list above.

The Bible tells us to be fishers of men (Mt 4:19). We are to go out and witness. We are to help train people up in Christ. Regardless how much we do this, we **cannot** appoint somebody to the position of apostle. Only Jesus can do this and he has not done it since he spoke to Saul & renamed him Paul (Acts 9).

Some may say, "But what of Matthias? Wasn't he appointed to the office of apostle so that the empty spot left by Judas would be filled? While this is an interesting point on the surface, we need look no further than Luke's words to see what really happened.

Acts 1:21-25

> "Therefore it is necessary that of the men who have accompanied us all the time that the Lord Jesus went in and out among us—beginning with the baptism of John until the day that He was taken up from us—one of these must become a witness with us of His

> resurrection." So they put forward two men, Joseph called Barsabbas (who was also called Justus), and Matthias. And they prayed and said, "You, Lord, who know the hearts of all men, show which one of these two **You have chosen** to occupy this ministry and apostleship from which Judas turned aside to go to his own place."

Notice the part in bold. It does not say, "Show us which one of these two You choose this day." It is written in the past tense. Matthias was not some afterthought. He was chosen by Jesus from the beginning. The decision was already made. Matthias was already chosen. His delayed entry in no way makes him a substitutionary candidate. In fact, one should argue as to whether or not Judas was ever a true apostle of Jesus Christ. I would argue that he was not and that Matthias was actually the true possessor of the title the whole time. He knew Jesus (v.21), witnessed the resurrection (v.22), and was chosen by Christ Himself (v.24).

Let's go back to the verses mentioned earlier in Ephesians. The whole reason for apostles (and prophets for that matter) was to lay the foundation of the Church. The Church was still in its infant stages. God called certain individuals, as He saw fit, to fill these offices. We already know the purpose of an apostle was to proclaim the Gospel of Jesus Christ and minister to the Jews and Gentiles. A prophet was called to relay a message from God. While teachers have a special ability to interpret the existing Word of God and teach others, a prophet had the special ability to proclaim a new Word from God. This Word would have been previously unknown. Again, these "miracle gifts" existed for the purpose of the advancement of the early Church. Through these signs, wonders, and miracles, apostles and prophets were able to show the people the power of God and the wondrous Truth of the Gospel.

We know Jesus founded the Church. In Matthew he says he will build it. Jesus is also the head of the Church. Jesus is the chief cornerstone. The use of apostles & prophets were to lay the foundation. They were used to get the Church started.

Basic construction knowledge will teach us that a foundation is what a building rests on. Without a solid foundation, a building will crumble (Luke 6:49). A solid foundation is vital to the survival of the building in times of trouble (Luke 6:48). It is very clear that apostles & prophets were used to lay the foundation. It should be noted that the apostles and prophets alone are not the foundation. It was through their signs, wonders, and miracles, granted by God Himself, that the foundation was laid. All of this was done with Christ in mind. Christ is the true foundation. He is the chief cornerstone. A cornerstone is the stone that sets the foundation. The entire building, including the foundation, rests upon the cornerstone. Therefore, Ephesians tells us that the apostles and prophets laid the foundation of the Church on Christ himself. Without Christ, the foundation is weak. It is as the man who built his house with no foundation at all. Jesus is the Rock in which our foundation is built.

Want to hear another interesting tidbit of information regarding construction? A building can only have one foundation. Once the foundation is laid, construction of the building commences. If the foundation is strong, it will never be laid again. Paul says the foundation has already been laid. He wrote it in the past tense. The Church is built on the foundation of the apostles and prophets but Christ is the foundation (cornerstone) that holds everything together for all eternity. Jesus has not come back and appointed anybody to lay a brand new foundation. To believe otherwise is unbiblical.

The Greek word for apostle is *apostolos*. The literal meaning of this word is "one sent forth." It is argued that since the word is used to describe others (Barnabas and Silas for example), the term is not to be used today. The term was also used in a broad sense to describe one who was sent with the power and authority of the apostles of Christ however, these men were not actual apostles of Christ. In the strict sense of the term, and the usage this chapter defines, apostle was limited to the original twelve as well as the special case of Paul. Timothy was sent by Paul but nowhere is he referred to as an apostle.

Teaching, pastoring, and evangelism (Ephesians 4:11) are examples of gifts that are used today to further build and advance the church and the Word of God. Now that the foundation has been laid, we are called to be pillars and support of the Truth (1 Tim 3:15). Just as you would build the pillars and walls of a building to help support it once the foundation has been laid, we are called to support the Truth of the Gospel built upon the solid Rock of Christ.

2 COULD JESUS SIN?

This is a topic that has been brought up many times over the years. There are always two sides with two totally different views. One side believes that since Jesus was a man, he could sin but chose not to. The other side believes that since Jesus was God, he could not sin at all. On which side do you stand at this very moment? Maybe you have never thought about it before now. My goal is that you will have formed your opinion by the end of this chapter.

First, let's start with the basics. Jesus was fully man. Man can sin (Romans 3:23). Jesus was also fully God. God and sin are total opposites. It is impossible for God to sin. This almost seems like a paradox. Stay with me for a minute.

Jesus was 100% man just as he was also 100% God. Scripture refers to God as being Light and says there is no darkness found in Him (1 John 1:5). This only makes sense. You turn on a light switch and the darkness flees. In much the same way, God cannot exist in the same place as sin. They are total opposites. Where God is, sin is not. Obviously, God is omnipresent (Psalm 139:7-10) so I am not referring to His physical location as much as I am His relationship with the person being tempted to sin. We know Jesus did not sin but it is just as accurate to say he could not sin either. In the Old Testament, a man was required to sacrifice his best animal to God. He would select an animal without any blemishes at all and sacrifice its flesh. In the same way, Christ was used as sinless flesh to be a sacrifice. His whole purpose for life was to destroy the works of the devil (1 John 3:8). The method he would accomplish this by was to die on the cross. He was the ultimate sacrifice. He was the flesh that beat the world. He was the flesh that Satan had no control over. Satan tried and failed miserably because he had no hold. This was one piece of flesh that could not sin because it was also 100% God.

Some will say he could have sinned because he was fully man but he did not because he was fully God. That is the same as saying God can sin but He chooses not to because of who He is. God cannot sin because it is against the very nature of who He is. That means if God cannot sin, Jesus did not merely **choose** not to sin. It means he was incapable of sinning. God does not just choose not to sin. He simply can't. I truly believe Jesus could not have sinned. People say he could have but didn't but that means God can but chooses not to. Most people would consider the latter to be blasphemy so why don't they say the same about the former? Jesus either is God or he isn't. If Jesus had been capable of sinning and, in his capability, did sin, would he stop being God? The answer is a resounding yes as God cannot sin. As he was God, he did not sin. Just as he could never stop being God, he not only never would have sinned but he would have been incapable of sinning. Yes, he was a man. Man can sin. Man also is not God. Jesus was both. Sorry, but God wins out over the flesh in every instance including this one. Jesus was flesh natured in the sense that he was a human but he was lacking sin because he was also God and God is on the complete opposite side of the spectrum from sin. When I say flesh natured, do not confuse this with a sinful nature. Human nature and sin nature are not always glued together. Where Adam was prone to failure, Jesus was not. He was in full communion with God as the perfect man because He was also our perfect God.

To understand this doctrine, one must understand what defines a man. Is it the ability to sin which defines man? Is it a fallen nature? Neither of these defines humanity. It is our flesh which defines us. Can one claim a stillborn is less human than a healthy baby? Certainly not! Just because one does not sin does not make him an alien. Jesus could not sin but this did not make him any less of a man. He was flesh through and through.

One argument that always comes up is the issue of temptation. Some will ask why Satan bothered to tempt Jesus in the wilderness (Matthew 4:1-11) if he could not have sinned. Satan had to have known he could not beat God yet he (and a third of the angels) attempted anyway. I believe history was repeating itself and Satan was trying to get Jesus to fall but because sin is so far removed from God, he could not sin. It is a prime example of flesh stomping Satan at his own game. He knows he can't win but he is going to try to cause as much of a disruption as possible. While Satan is not omniscient, he was created by God for the purpose of serving God. As a result, while not being omniscient, it is safe to assume he knew of God's might as he was around when the heavens and earth were created. He was a first hand witness to God's omnipotence.

We are to follow Jesus and strive to be like him but that does not mean Jesus had to have been able to sin. In the Old Testament, people were to follow God's commands and remain pure. They did not have Jesus to follow. They only had their faith in God. God could not sin yet they were to follow Him anyway. The same goes for Jesus. Jesus could not have sinned (because he was also fully God) but we are still to follow him. Following Jesus is the same as following God's commands. It just takes it a step further by allowing us a way to be reconciled to God.

Let's go back to the story of Jesus being tempted by Satan in the wilderness. Some say if Jesus could have been tempted, he must have at least had the ability to sin. On the other hand, I have said that since Jesus **was** God, there was no way he could have sinned.

> **Mark 1:13**
>
> And He was in the wilderness forty days being tempted by Satan; and He was with the wild beasts, and the angels were ministering to Him.

Many of you will admit that God could not sin yet you claim that since Jesus was tempted, he could. How is it that God was tempted yet not able to sin?

> **Psalm 106:14**
>
> But craved intensely in the wilderness,
> And tempted God in the desert.

Compare the words used in the original Hebrew and Greek.

OT Usage
nacah - הסנ
1) to test, try, prove, tempt, assay, put to the proof or test

NT Usage
peirazō - πειράζω
1) to try whether a thing can be done
a) to attempt, endeavour
2) to try, make trial of, test: for the purpose of ascertaining his quantity, or what he thinks, or how he will behave himself

Temptation does not affect one unless their heart is outside of God's Will. Temptation will only affect one with a sinful nature. As a teenager, I used to think Jesus would have had this sinful nature being born of man. Well, if you think about it, Jesus was not born with a spirit of man. He was conceived and born from the Spirit of God (Matthew 1:18-20). This would not carry with it the same sinful nature that mankind possesses but it does not make Jesus any less of a man. If temptation held no power over Jesus, it technically was not true temptation at all. It was more of an attempt to tempt. His heart was always in the right place so temptation could never have been any more than weak attempts to him.

As a man, Jesus should have had the ability to sin but since he was born from the Spirit of God (& in actuality **was** God), he could not have sinned because temptation was so far removed from him that it made it impossible. Satan put him to the test. Jesus passed with flying colors just as God did when the nation of Israel tempted Him. This does not mean either could have fallen into sin. It simply means they did not. Gee, I wonder why.

3 RULES TO LIVE BY

Our society is governed by rules. There are rules everywhere. We have speed limits. We have emissions. We have dress codes. Rules are the very foundation of almost everything we do in life. When we see a cop in our rearview mirror, we tend to be overcome by a certain sense of fear and we immediately look at the speedometer. This is a healthy fear of one who holds our money and driving privileges in his hands. Why are we not this way when it comes to God?

When we break one of the laws put in place by human authorities, we look over our shoulder. When we break one of the laws put in place by the very One who created everything, most don't even bat an eye. Do we feel God isn't watching? Do we feel He doesn't care? Perhaps we feel like nothing will happen to us and that we will get away with it.

While almost everybody has heard of the Ten Commandments, not everybody fully understands them. Many people take them as general guidelines for life as if they are merely for personal gain. This is utter blasphemy! It equates God with nothing more than an advisor. While I do not plan on going over all of them, I would like to touch on a few.

Exodus 20:3-4

> You shall have no other gods before Me. You shall not make for yourself an idol, or any likeness of what is in heaven above or on the earth beneath or in the water under the earth.

Many Christians violate this day in and day out without ever realizing it. We do this with our cars, money, work, play, etc. We even do this with our sleep. Simply put, an idol is anything we place above God.

Jesus gave up his life for us but we are often too tired to wake up for church on Sunday morning. In the Navy, I have the privilege of praying on the ship's intercom at night. While it is definitely a privilege, it can also become burdensome after a short while. I'm guilty of being tempted to go to sleep early and not do this evening prayer on some nights but I know that is the selfishness in me trying to overcome God. Sleep is important and God will forgive me if I choose to go to bed instead. However, just because God will forgive me, it doesn't necessarily mean it is the best choice? I've found that if it will lead to me having to ask forgiveness of God, it probably isn't the best choice to begin with.

Exodus 20:7

> You shall not take the name of the LORD your God in vain, for the LORD will not leave him unpunished who takes His name in vain.

Walk the streets or halls of work and count the number of times you hear somebody taking the Lord's name in vain. It is indeed sickening. I hear everything ranging from someone simply muttering the name of Jesus for no good reason, all the way to someone cursing someone on God's behalf. If we say the name of God, there needs to be a reason; no ifs, ands, or buts. To say the name of God without a Godly intent is to take His name in vain. To curse someone or something on God's behalf is even worse because it is assuming the role of God and laying judgment. In fact, the Jewish community takes the name of God so seriously that they do not even spell it out for fear of it being defaced or used irreverently. As a substitute, they go to such lengths as to write it out as "G-d" out of fear, honor, and love.

Furthermore, how often have you heard someone "swear to God" in order to convey a sense of authenticity when speaking? This one is probably thought of less than any other because most people think if they are being honest, there is no harm.

James 5:12

> But above all, my brethren, do not swear, either by heaven or by earth or with any other oath; but your yes is to be your yes, and your no, no, so that you may not fall under judgment.

Matthew 5:37

> But let your statement be, 'Yes, yes' or 'No, no'; anything beyond these is of evil.

Clearly, this is not saying that all swearing to God is prohibited, as exhibited in multiple Scripture references (Genesis 24:2-3; Joshua 2:12; Exodus 22:10-11). What Jesus and James are getting at is frivolous swearing and oath-taking. In most cases, one's yes is to be yes and his no to be no. We are not to casually swear to God for the sake of making someone believe us. Swearing to God is not a gimmick. It is a solemn oath before our Lord and is to be used with careful discretion and reservation.

Matthew 7:1

> Do not judge so that you will not be judged.

Judgment belongs to God and God alone. Who are we to assume such a role? Despite this, I hear it coming out of the mouths of Christians all the time. It is almost as if they are not even thinking about it. I can guarantee you they are not praising God most of the time. They are breaking the third commandment of God. Again, why do we not even so much as bat an eye when it happens? Why do we not fear God?

Exodus 20:13

> You shall not murder.

Many people take this verse and recite it as, "You shall not kill." This has been used by anti-military types who claim the military should not exist. The Hebrew word used for murder is *ratsach* and is used only 4 times in the Old Testament. It is a general word that implies any kind of killing be it on purpose or accidental. However, we also see many places in Scripture where God actually commands Israel to kill everyone in a village and to spare no one. We have to look at the context.

Dr. J. Vernon McGee

> The commandment "Thou shalt not kill" was *not* given to a nation; it was given to the individual. "Thou shalt not kill" has nothing to do with soldier service or with the execution of a criminal. A nation is given an authority to protect human life by taking human life.[1]

Based on the Greek as well as the proper context, we can see that the blanket statement that there should be no military is not supported in Scripture as some contend. It was a command to individuals. However, does it stop with literal murder or is there more to this command of God?

Genesis 37:4-5 & 8

> His brothers saw that their father loved him more than all his brothers; and so they hated him and could not speak to him on friendly terms. Then Joseph had a dream, and when he told it to his brothers, they hated him even more. Then his brothers said to him, "Are you actually going to reign over us? Or are you really going to rule over us?" So they hated him even more for his dreams and for his words.

This is a perfect example of a family feud gone overboard. Joseph was much loved by his father. In fact, Scripture is very clear that Israel loved him more so than his brothers. This became such a point of contention that Joseph's brothers, in their hatred, conspired to kill him. If we continue to read the story of Joseph, we see that their plan failed and Joseph rose to a prestigious position under the Pharaoh. Does this mean their murder plot would be reduced to nothing more than a conspiracy to commit murder when held on trial in God's court?

Matthew 5:21-22

> You have heard that the ancients were told, 'YOU SHALL NOT COMMIT MURDER' and 'Whoever commits murder shall be liable to the court.' But I say to you that **everyone who is angry with his brother shall be guilty** before the court;

1 John 3:15

> Everyone who hates his brother is a murderer; and you know that no murderer has eternal life abiding in him.

How often do we find ourselves committing murder? How often do we commit a wrongdoing against someone simply because we are annoyed by them or dislike them? As far as God is concerned, this is murder. If Scripture has already warned us that everyone who is angry with his brother shall be found guilty, why do we not even bat an eye?

Exodus 20:14

> You shall not commit adultery.

Ask a group of people to break this one down and you will probably get the same answer. Most people take it to mean monogamy. While this is indeed one meaning, and many people are guilty of it, it is not the only meaning.

Matthew 5:27-28

> You have heard that it was said, 'YOU SHALL NOT COMMIT ADULTERY'; but I say to you that **everyone who looks at a woman with lust for her has already committed adultery** with her in his heart.

While I would hope none of you reading have ever cheated on our spouses by being with another woman or man physically, according to Scripture, mentally cheating is just as bad. The Greek word used for "looks" is *blepo*. The usage in verse 28 does not refer to an "accidental" glance. While lustful thoughts may pop into our mind by even just a glance, the context implies much more than this. It implies a continuous stare with the intention of lustful thoughts. If one stares at another, be they the opposite sex or the same, with the intention of lusting, adultery is not *currently* being committed. It says it has **already** happened in the heart. All sin stems from a sinful nature within us. If we look with lust, it is because our heart is vile and we fall prey to it. However, Christ has given us a new nature. We are no longer bound by our fallen heart. We have an option to turn away and not entertain it. It is not easy by any stretch of the imagination but it is still possible.

Job 31:1

> I made a covenant with my eyes not to look lustfully at a girl.

A.W. Pink

> If lustful looking is so grievous a sin, then those who dress and expose themselves with the desire to be looked at and lusted after…are not less but perhaps more guilty. In this matter it is not only too often the case that men sin but women tempt them to do so. How great ten must be the guilt of the great majority of modern misses who deliberately seek to arouse the sexual passions of young men. And how much greater still is the guilt of most of their mothers for allowing them to become lascivious temptresses.[ii]

As I said at the beginning, the Ten Commandments are well known by almost everybody although they are rarely understood in their full context. We only touched 4 of the 10. Ask yourselves how many of them you routinely fall short on. One can understand all of the Ten Commandments yet still fall short of, what I believe to be, one of the greatest commandments ever given.

1 Corinthians 1:31

> So that, just as it is written, "LET HIM WHO BOASTS, **BOAST IN THE LORD**."

Have you ever boasted in the Lord? This is not something that most Christians live up to. We often boast about how we earned a promotion for our hard work. We boast about how we helped a group of people at church. We even boast about how much time we spend reading our Bibles. While all of these are great things, none of them are worthy of boasting.

Galatians 6:14a

> But may it never be that I would boast, except in the cross of our Lord Jesus Christ,

As Christians, we are commanded to do far more than observe the Ten Commandments. The Ten Commandments are indeed to be observed but we have a much higher calling.

Matthew 4:19

> And he said to them, "Follow Me and I will make you **fishers of men**."

Matthew 28:19

> Go therefore and **make disciples of all nations**, baptizing them in the name of the Father and the Son and the Holy Spirit

1 Corinthians 1:23a

> But we **preach Christ crucified**

Matthew 22:36-39

> "Teacher, which is the great commandment in the Law?" And He said to him, " 'YOU SHALL LOVE THE LORD YOUR GOD WITH ALL YOUR HEART, AND WITH ALL YOUR SOUL, AND WITH ALL YOUR MIND.' This is the great and foremost commandment. The second is like it, 'YOU SHALL LOVE YOUR NEIGHBOR AS YOURSELF.' "

We are called to worship and servitude. Too often, we become complacent and forget what God has called us to do. He has not called us simply to be good. He has not called us simply to love Him. He has called us to serve Him. How can we serve Him if we don't even know what He wants us to do for Him? Thankfully, it is all outlined in His Word. He wants us to be out there teaching others. A fisherman does not sit idly as the fish swim by. They are actively casting their nets in an attempt to catch the fish. While we can do no catching of our own, if we allow God to work through us, you would be amazed what can happen! We are called to make disciples of all nations. How can we make disciples if we don't even preach the Gospel to the lost? We are called to preach Christ crucified. Without the Truth of the death & resurrection of Christ, there is no hope. With this knowledge, why are we so casual about people moving closer and closer to eternal death? Even more so, why are we so casual about breaking the laws of God? How can we go day by day breaking His commands and walking in our own without so much as even batting an eye?

If you have found yourself in any of these situations, I urge you to follow 1 Corinthians 1:2.

1 Corinthians 1:2

> To the church of God which is at Corinth, to those who have been sanctified in Christ Jesus, saints by calling, with all who in every place **call on the name of our Lord Jesus Christ**, their Lord and ours:

Call on the name of our Lord Jesus Christ and ask him to guide you in your walk. Ask him to show you how to live. Ask him to help you follow his laws. Ask him to truly be the Lord that you claim him to be by following the laws he has commanded you walk in.

[i] J. Vernon McGee, Genesis-Deuteronomy Commentary (Vol I), [Nashville, TN by Thomas Nelson, Inc., 1981], Pg. 268

[ii] A.W. Pink, An Exposition of the Sermon on the Mount [Grand Rapids: Baker, 1974], pg. 83

4 LEGALISM VS. LICENSE

In chapter 3, I spoke on our insensitivity to the commands of God. We get the scare of a lifetime when caught by a cop but do not even so much as bat an eye when we know full and well we are already caught by God. The Bible has many examples of God punishing violators of His commands with the punishment of death yet even this does not make us blink. While God has His standards and His commands, we can be thankful that we also share in His love. It is His love that provides a certain sense of liberty.

John 8:36

> So if the Son makes you free, you will be free indeed.

Christ has set us free. How can we so boldly make this assertion? It is because we can trust the Scriptures which so plainly say so.

John 14:6a

> Jesus said to him, "I am the way, and **the truth**, and the life;

John 8:32

> and you will know **the truth**, and **the truth** will make you free.

All men desire freedom. Dating back to the days of slavery, freedom has been something that is deeply sought after. In a Christian sense, there is only one way to that freedom and that is the Son, the Truth. Christ is the Truth and all who know the Truth will be free.

This freedom covers a few basic areas. The first we will touch on is the area of freedom from sin. Before Christ, we were all slaves to sin. We were all victims to the bondage of sin. We were bound by the chains of sin.

John 8:34

> Jesus answered them, "Truly, truly, I say to you, everyone who commits sin is the slave of sin.

What is a slave? A slave is one who is bound to obey the will of his master. He has no say in and of himself. He simply follows orders. He is owned by his master. John not only says we get caught up in sin but goes so far as to say we were slaves to sin. Paul reiterates this fact in Romans 6:6. In fact, John states if anybody commits a sin at all, he is a slave to sin.

Romans 3:23

> for all have sinned and fall short of the glory of God,

Not a single one of us can make the claim that we are free from imperfection. We are all guilty of sin. It is just in our nature to fall. There is only one man in history to have ever lived a sinless life and that is our Savior, Jesus Christ. According to John, which really means according to God as it is His written Word, even one sin makes us a slave to sin. Not only are we a slave to sin but we have no desire to turn from it.

John 3:20

> For everyone who does evil hates the Light, and does not come to the Light for fear that his deeds will be exposed.

John 8:44a

> You are of your father the devil, and you want to do the desires of your father

Slaves to sin are at war with God and serve Satan willingly. Slaves to sin hate God and want to do the desires of Satan much like a drug addict willingly comes back for another "fix" time and time again. Satan does not set us free. He is the one who keeps his slaves bound. It is only through the Son that one can be set free, and as we already covered…

John 8:36

> So if the Son makes you free, you will be free indeed.

Galatians 5:1

> It was for freedom that Christ set us free; therefore keep standing firm and do not be subject again to a yoke of slavery.

It is in Christ alone that we finally have our freedom.

Romans 8:2

For the law of the Spirit of life in **Christ Jesus has set you free** from the law of sin and of death.

Romans 3:27-28

Where then is boasting? It is excluded. By what kind of law? Of works? No, but by a law of faith. For we maintain that a man is justified by faith apart from works of the Law.

Romans 7:12-13

So then, the Law is holy, and the commandment is holy and righteous and good. Therefore did that which is good become a cause of death for me? May it never be! Rather it was sin, in order that it might be shown to be sin by effecting my death through that which is good, that through the commandment sin might become utterly sinful.

We can see the Law is not to blame. The Law simply pointed out our sin. If there is no Law, one can never be guilty. The law of God is referred to as the law of sin and death because man is sinful and it points out exactly that. It is Christ who gives us freedom from the Old Testament law and gives us hope in faith.

Romans 6:14

For sin shall not be master over you, for you are not under law, but under grace.

2 Corinthians 3:17

> Now the Lord is the Spirit; and where the Spirit of the Lord is, there is liberty.

The commands of God are not merely suggestions. They are orders from Almighty God and they are to be followed. There are some religions out there who claim that if you follow these commands, you will go to Heaven. In fact, many claim that just by being a "good" person, you will go to Heaven. A common theme in my lessons recently has been salvation in Christ alone. Even though God has commands that are to be followed, they will not save.

Acts 15:1 & 10-11

> Some men came down from Judea and began teaching the brethren, "Unless you are circumcised according to the custom of Moses, you cannot be saved."......... "Now therefore why do you put God to the test by placing upon the neck of the disciples a yoke which neither our fathers nor we have been able to bear? But we believe that we are saved through the grace of the Lord Jesus, in the same way as they also are."

Even if it were possible to follow all the commands of God, which it isn't (Romans 3:23), we would still be in the same predicament we were in before we came to know Christ; slaves to sin. However, in Christ we have a sense of freedom. We have a sense of liberty.

1 John 2:1

> My little children, I am writing these things to you so that you may not sin And if anyone sins, we have an Advocate with the Father, Jesus Christ the righteous;

Commands are to be followed but when we fail, we can rest assured that we have an Advocate with the Father. Christ steps in the place of any judgment that would have come to us and allows us to remain in the Father. In fact, Christ is the One who secures our place with the Father and ensures we will never lose it. It is because we are not under the law of the Spirit of life that we have liberty. We are free to enjoy the things of life without fear of judgment.

On the other hand, liberty is not the same as license. While not being bound to the law, we still have obligations. For instance, we are not to be a stumbling block to others.

1 Corinthians 8:7-13

> However not all men have this knowledge; but some, being accustomed to the idol until now, eat food as if it were sacrificed to an idol; and their conscience being weak is defiled. But food will not commend us to God; we are neither the worse if we do not eat, nor the better if we do eat. But take care that this liberty of yours does not somehow become a stumbling block to the weak. For if someone sees you, who have knowledge, dining in an idol's temple, will not his conscience, if he is weak, be strengthened to eat things sacrificed to idols? For through your knowledge he who is weak is ruined, the brother for whose sake Christ died. And so, by sinning against the brethren and wounding their conscience when it is weak, you sin against Christ. Therefore, if food causes my brother to stumble, I will never eat meat again, so that I will not cause my brother to stumble.

This was written during a time when sacrifices to idols were common practice. The meat being sacrificed to idols was perfectly fine meat. In fact, it was some of the best meat because the pagans wanted to give their gods the best. Just as in Elijah's day, not a thing happened with the meat offered to idols because their "gods" were just as lifeless as the meat they sacrificed to them.

1 Kings 18:21-27

> Elijah came near to all the people and said, "How long will you hesitate between two opinions? If the LORD is God, follow Him; but if Baal, follow him." But the people did not answer him a word. Then Elijah said to the people, "I alone am left a prophet of the LORD, but Baal's prophets are 450 men. Now let them give us two oxen; and

> let them choose one ox for themselves and cut it up, and place it on the wood, but put no fire under it; and I will prepare the other ox and lay it on the wood, and I will not put a fire under it. Then you call on the name of your god, and I will call on the name of the LORD, and the God who answers by fire, He is God." And all the people said, "That is a good idea." So Elijah said to the prophets of Baal, "Choose one ox for yourselves and prepare it first for you are many, and call on the name of your god, but put no fire under it." Then they took the ox which was given them and they prepared it and called on the name of Baal from morning until noon saying, "O Baal, answer us." But there was no voice and no one answered. And they leaped about the altar which they made. It came about at noon, that Elijah mocked them and said, "Call out with a loud voice, for he is a god; either he is occupied or gone aside, or is on a journey, or perhaps he is asleep and needs to be awakened."

Elijah's was a funny man. Elijah was completely bashing their false god by going so far as to say he might be currently occupied. The Hebrew word used for occupied is *siyg* which implies a private place. In other words, Elijah was saying Baal might not be answering because he was busy using the bathroom. He was not surprised that nothing happened with the offered ox. In the same way, in 1 Corinthians, Paul was pointing out that there is nothing wrong with the meat offered up to idols. It was some of the best stuff out there and after the sacrifices, it was put up for sale in the markets. Newer Christians who were weak in their faith would turn away from this meat because of the negative connotation it held. Stronger Christians knew this was some of the best stuff and had no fear in purchasing it because of their liberty in Christ. Technically speaking, they had every right to eat that meat. It had no power as it was offered up to nothing. That was all the false gods amounted to; absolute nothingness. The meat was as good as any. However, this was becoming a problem. The liberty of the stronger Christians was becoming a stumbling block to the faith of the weaker Christians. It was going against their very conscience.

John MacArthur uses a great analogy to explain the difference between the liberty of a mature Christian and the restrictions of an immature Christian.

John MacArthur

> A small child is not allowed to play with sharp tools, to go into the street, or to go where there are dangerous machines or electrical appliances. The restrictions are gradually removed as he grows older and learns for himself what is dangerous and what is not. God confines His spiritual children by conscience. As they grow in knowledge and maturity the limits of conscience are expanded. We should never expand our actions and habits before our conscience permits it. And we should never encourage, either directly or indirectly, anyone else to do that.[i]

Not only are we to not be a stumbling block to others but we are also not to try to be our own spiritual version of James Bond. He had a license to kill. We do not have a license to kill nor do we have a license to sin.

Romans 6:1-2a

> What shall we say then? Are we to continue in sin so that grace may increase? May it never be!

Romans 6:15

> What then? Shall we sin because we are not under law but under grace? May it never be!

1 Peter 2:16

> Act as free men, and do not use your freedom as a covering for evil, but use it as bondslaves of God.

We are never to use liberty as license. There is a fine line that must be followed. We are to follow the commands of God while also honoring our liberty in Christ. To neglect God's commands is to act as if He does not matter. To neglect our liberty in Christ is to act as if Christ is not all sufficient regarding our salvation. Both Paul and James give very good instruction on how to walk that fine line comfortably.

Galatians 5:13

> For you were called to freedom, brethren; only do not turn your freedom into an opportunity for the flesh, but through love serve one another.

Galatians 5:16

> But I say, walk by the Spirit, and you will not carry out the desire of the flesh.

James 1:25

> But one who looks intently at the perfect law, the law of liberty, and abides by it, not having become a forgetful hearer but an effectual doer, this man will be blessed in what he does.

Love God. Worship God. Obey God. Have liberty in Christ but never abuse it to the point of using it as license. The law of liberty does not give us liberty to sin at will. It gives us liberty to obey a God that we were incapable of obeying while in a state of hatred towards Him. Walk in the Spirit, become an effectual doer of the Word, and take comfort in the Advocacy of Christ in our eternal reconciliation to the Father.

---

[i] John MacArthur, The MacArthur New Testament Commentary on First Corinthians [Moody Publishers, 1984] pg. 196

5 DOES GOD HATE THE SIN OR THE SINNER?

God has many attributes. He is loving. He is kind. He is good. He is righteous. He is strong. He is almighty. He is everlasting. The attributes of God are eternal aspects of Him that do not sway to one side or the other based on external circumstances. Many people take these attributes and forget another aspect of God. While God has His unswaying attributes, He also has His traits. The trait we are going to focus on in this chapter is the hatred of God.

Hatred is not an attribute of God. As we discussed, an attribute is something that does not vary depending on an external force. God is all loving but He is not all hating. However, just because He is not all hating does not mean He cannot hate. God's hatred is but one of His many traits. His hatred is not all defining but is rather in response to the existence of sin. If sin were to not exist, God's love would remain but His hatred would not. As I said, we are going to discuss His hatred. We are specifically going to cover the topic of God's hatred toward not just sin but toward the actual sinner.

We have all heard the saying, "God loves the sinner but hates the sin." While it sounds nice and tickles the ears, have we ever really thought to stop and question this age old Sunday School teaching? I am here to say confidently that God does hate sin but he also **does** hate the sinner. God does not hate the sinner just for the sake of hating him. He hates the sinner because of the sin found in him. I know many of you are probably scratching your head and saying that is unbiblical but look at the following verses:

Proverbs 6:16-19

> There are six things which the LORD hates,
> Yes, seven which are an abomination to Him:
> Haughty eyes, a lying tongue,
> And hands that shed innocent blood,
> heart that devises wicked plans,
> Feet that run rapidly to evil,
> A false witness who utters lies,
> And one who spreads strife among brothers.

Psalm 5:5

> The boastful shall not stand before Your eyes;
> You hate all who do iniquity.

Psalm 11:5

> The LORD tests the righteous and the wicked,
> And the one who loves violence His soul hates.

God does indeed hate sinners. Those verses listed above are not about God hating the sin in the world. They are clearly talking about sinners. We were all sinners at one point. We were all lost. We were all spiritually dead and separated from God.

Romans 3:23

> for all have sinned and fall short of the glory of God,

Thankfully, God loved us enough to send His son to die on the cross so that we could be reconciled to Him. Right about now you might be asking yourself how God could possibly love someone enough to die for them yet hate them at the same time. This would certainly be a confusing contradiction at best. Thankfully, this is not the case at all and, as we venture further, it should become clear as to why.

Romans 5:6-10

> For while we were still helpless, at the right time **Christ died for the ungodly**. For one will hardly die for a righteous man; though perhaps for the good man someone would dare even to die. But **God demonstrates His own love toward us, in that while we were yet sinners, Christ died for us**. Much more then, having now been justified by His blood, we shall be saved from the wrath of God through Him. For if **while we were enemies we were reconciled to God through the death of His Son**, much more, having been reconciled, we shall be saved by His life.

People often use this passage (in conjunction with John 3:16) to say God loves everybody in the world. This simply is not the case. If it were, the verses I posted above would be lying to us. God cannot love everybody and hate people at the same time. It is not possible. Paul was speaking to believers in the book of Romans.

Romans 1:6-7

> among whom you also are the called of Jesus Christ; to all who are beloved of God in Rome, called as saints: Grace to you and peace

> from God our Father and the Lord Jesus Christ.

We cannot apply these words to the world because Paul specifically states they are for believers in Christ. What can we draw from Romans 5:6-10?

1) Christ died for the ungodly
2) while **we** were yet **sinners** Christ died for **us**
3) **we** shall be saved from the wrath of God

John 3:16a

> For God so loved the world, that He gave His only begotten Son

This is a very true statement. God loved the world. We were once in the world. He loved **us** in the world enough to offer a way to bring us back to Him. That way was through His Son. Christ did not die for everybody in the world. He died for us while we were still in the world. He died so that we may be able to come out of the world, die to ourselves, and become a new creature in Christ (2 Corinthians 5:17). At this point, we are saved from the wrath of God.

I do not believe God hated us while we were still sinners. Romans 5:8 tells us that God loved us while we were still sinners. If God hates all sinners, how is this possible? It is because God does not hate all sinners. Psalm 5:5 says God hates all who do iniquity yet Romans 3:23 says we all fall into this category. The "all" in Psalm 5:5 is referring to those characterized by their iniquity much like 1 John 3:10 does the same. It is not saying God hates all who sin but rather, all who are characterized by said sin. He hates those whom He has not called to Himself. It is the ones that God has no intention of calling that He hates. Yes, He hates them. Read the first 3 verses I gave if you still do not believe God hates anyone. Again, God does not hate all sinners (because He loved us while we were still sinners) but He does very much so hate the rest of the sinners of this world. Some call it cold, cruel, selfish, arrogant, prejudiced, etc. The reality of it is that it is totally just. As I said in the beginning, this is not because of whom the person is but because of the sin found within him.

How can I possibly back this up? I find Romans 9 helps to clear it up and put things in a proper perspective.

Romans 9:18-24

> So then He has mercy on whom He desires, and He hardens whom He desires. You will say to me then, "Why does He still find fault? For who resists His will?" On the contrary, who are you, O man, who answers back to God? The thing molded will not say to the molder, "Why did you make me like this," will it? Or does not the potter have a right over the clay, to make from the same lump one vessel for honorable use and another for common use? What if God, although willing to demonstrate His wrath and to make His power known, endured with much patience vessels of wrath prepared for destruction? And He did so to make known the riches of His glory upon vessels of mercy, which He prepared beforehand for glory, even us, whom He also called, not from among Jews only, but also from among Gentiles.

I do not believe the love of God is relevant to all. We are merely clay. God is the potter. Before the foundation of the world, He chose some to be vessels fitted unto honor. He chose others to be vessels fitted unto common use. The King James Version renders the latter as "dishonour." God has His purpose. God has His Will. God has His plans. Who are we to question how He has made us or what He has made us into? Who are we to question God if He chooses to harden our heart?

Psalm 14:2-3

> The LORD has looked down from heaven upon the sons of men to see if there are any who understand, who seek after God. They have all turned aside, together they have become corrupt; There is no one who does good, not even one.

Nobody seeks after God with their own heart (Psalm 14:2-3). It is only the elect that God ordained before the foundation of the world that He loves. Yes, they are sinners but they are sinners that fall under God's love. It is at this time only that the love of God even comes into play. Before this point, we were all merely clay.

There are some out there who take random verses to try to disprove the existence of the hatred of God toward anybody. They try to say that God loves all unconditionally and that His hatred does not exist. They take single verses to go as far as to claim that none will go to Hell and that all will be saved. We will speak more on this subject in chapter 15. These people quote verses such as 2 Peter 3:9 in an attempt to prove their claims.

2 Peter 3:9

> The Lord is not slow about His promise, as some count slowness, but is patient toward <u>you</u>, not wishing for any to perish but for all to come to repentance.

That verse does not say anything about the call of God nor does it speak of all of humanity. It speaks of the Purpose of God.

The word used for the "wishing" is bou/lomai (*boulomai*)
The word most often used for the Call of God is kale/w (*kaleo*)

Boulomai is most often used when referring to the purposeful Will of God (Lk 22:42, Acts 5:28 & 33). It is not used to speak of general wants, desires or wishes. It is used to speak of decrees with purpose!

Even more, we must look at the verse and not just focus on the one word.

2 Peter 1:1

> Simon Peter, a bond-servant and apostle of Jesus Christ, To those who have received a faith of the same kind as ours, by the righteousness of our God and Savior, Jesus Christ:

Peter wrote this letter to the Church. What do we see in the verse shown above? I'll show it again:

2 Peter 3:9

> The Lord is not slow about His promise, as some count slowness, but is **patient toward you**, not wishing for any to perish but for all to come to repentance.

This verse is directed toward believers. It is encouragement for believers everywhere. It is reaffirming God's love toward us, the elect, whom He chose before the foundation of the world just as a potter forms clay. None of the elect from Romans 9 will perish (as we will cover in our next chapter).

Since we know the word *boulomai* is used to refer to God's purposeful Will, we can safely believe it is **not** saying God purposefully Wills that all will be saved and none go to Hell. Since the Greek here does not refer to the Call of God, we can safely believe it is not saying "all men are called but only certain ones are saved" as is a common belief of today. It says God purposefully Wills that none will perish.

How can this be if we know people will in fact perish? It is because Peter was not speaking of the entire world. He was speaking of and to believers. No believer will perish so be encouraged and have faith in the Truth. Peter is reassuring us, as believers, that God will not let us perish. We will not have to face His wrath.

Romans 5:8

> But God demonstrates His own love toward us, in that while we were yet sinners, Christ died for us.

God demonstrated His love for us, in that while we were yet sinners, Christ died for us. We were still in the world when Christ died. We were lost. God demonstrated His love toward us and none of us, who are called by God, will perish. It is not speaking of the entire world. It is referring to us while we were still in the world as sinners.

While we are on the subject, let's break down 1 Peter 3:18:

1 Peter 3:18

> For Christ also died for sins once for all, the just for the unjust, in order that He might bring us to God, having been put to death in the flesh, but made alive in the spirit;

Just as the "us" in 2 Peter 3:8 refers to believers, it points to the same crowd in 1 Peter 3:18. The death of Christ was not in vain. It was to reconcile the elect of God. Christ died for the sins of us once and for all and we will not face his wrath or perish.

God does not hate all sinners. God does not hate those whom are His elect. God hates those that will be going to Hell. He does not hate sinners that will be called to Him. While we were yet sinners God demonstrated His love toward us. On the same token, those whom He has not elected, God does indeed hate and has promised to destroy with His wrath. This does not bring Him any pleasure (Ezekiel 33:11), as a God who is love can never find joy in hate, but it is something that He must do out of His justice which rides on His eternal decree.

Let's review what we have covered up until now:

1) The Bible gives specific details on the fact that God does indeed hate sinners.
2) The Bible says God has purposefully willed (not called) that none should perish. We know many will perish so we must either count the Bible as contradicting or we must seek to find the context. In this case, the context is believers.
3) Bible says God loved believers while we were yet sinners. It is still very clear that God hates any sinner whom He has not called.
4) Romans 9 says not all are called.

All **have** sinned. Yes, believers are inclusive in Romans 3:23. Even if you wanted to say Romans 3:23 must follow the same "us/we" rules and claim it is only referring to believers, we **know** unbelievers sin. This is why they are going to be judged by the wrath of God. Again, all of Scripture must be taken into account. The implication of "us" is indeed written in many verses while being directed toward believers only.

Romans 5:8

> But God demonstrates His own love toward us, in that while we were yet sinners, Christ died for us.

2 Peter 3:9

> The Lord is not slow about His promise, as some count slowness, but

> is patient toward you *(remember, it was written to believers)*, not wishing for any to perish but for all to come to repentance.

1 Peter 3:18

> For Christ also died for sins once for all, the just for the unjust, so that He might bring us to God, having been put to death in the flesh, but made alive in the spirit;

Now the question remains as to why Christ died for all sins if some people are not going to be covered. I don't believe he *did* die for all sins. I believe he died for all the sins of the ones that God has called or will call at some point in the future. As to whom those people are, we have no idea. We are to preach Christ crucified. We are to be a bondservant to God. He tells us to do it and we gladly accept the task on unconditional terms. A bondservant is in a state of constant servitude but it is not out of hate while only pretending to love. Slaves had the option of leaving their master after a certain amount of time had passed. They had the choice to leaving or they could stay with their master for life. This was a lifelong choice. There was no going back. There was no leaving this state of constant servitude should they change their minds down the road. A bondservant would stay with their master if they truly loved their life and their master took care of them. Mary is described as a bondservant of the Lord. She did not hate God while only pretending to love Him. She truly loved Him and was glad to be a servant to Him for the rest of her life. In this way, we give glory to God and He works through us when and how He chooses. Witness unconditionally and let God decide who He calls according to Romans 9.

While it may seem like God is nothing more than a Master to us, He is a Father to us as well. A bondservant gladly serves their master just as we gladly serve God. We are God's servants. He takes great care of us. He is also our Father who loves us (and showed it by sending His Son to die for us). However, both a bondservant and a child will reject the desires of their master/parent from time to time in a moment of iniquity. In return, both a master and a parent will correct their servant/child and get them back on the right path of servitude/obedience.

6 PREDESTINATION

Welcome to one of the most controversial subjects within the Christian faith: how is one saved? Is it by faith or is it by predestination? If God pre-destined us that would mean that He already chose us. There would be no choice on our part. However, the Bible also says by grace we are saved through faith. That seemingly implies that we have a choice. Are we choosing to save ourselves by believing in Christ or is He the one doing ALL the work in saving us?

Romans 9:20-24, KJV

> Nay but, O man, who art thou that repliest against God? Shall the thing formed say to Him that formed it, Why hast thou made me thus? Hath not the potter power over the clay, of the same lump to make one vessel unto honour, and another unto dishonour? What if God, willing to show His wrath, and to make His power known, endured with much longsuffering the vessels of wrath fitted to destruction: And that He might make known the riches of His glory on the vessels of mercy, which He had afore prepared unto glory, Even us, whom He hath called, not of the Jews only, but also of the Gentiles?

While I feel this passage clears up the doctrine of predestination, there are many who refuse to accept it as Truth. It is my attempt that by the end of the chapter, it will be as clear to you as it is to me.

Romans 8:28-30

> And we know that God causes all things to work together for good to those who love God, to those who are called according to His purpose. For those whom He foreknew, He also predestined to become conformed to the image of His Son, so that He would be the firstborn among many brethren; and these whom He predestined, He also called; and these whom He called, He also justified; and these whom He justified, He also glorified.

Ephesians 1:5-6

> just as He chose us in Him before the foundation of the world, that we would be holy and blameless before Him. In love He predestined us to adoption as sons through Jesus Christ to Himself, according to the kind intention of His will,

2 Timothy 1:9

> who has saved us and called us with a holy calling, not according to our works, but according to His own purpose and grace which was granted us in Christ Jesus from all eternity,

Some say these passages are not referring to Heaven or Hell but rather a predetermined role we will play in the Church. There is actually some truth to this. While the Scripture DOES speak on predestined salvation, there are also many verses which speak on our active roles within the body.

Jeremiah 1:5

> "Before I formed you in the womb I knew you,
>   And before you were born I consecrated you;

> I have appointed you a prophet to the nations."

Psalm 139:16

> Your eyes have seen my unformed substance;
>   And in Your book were all written
>   The days that were ordained for me,
>   When as yet there was not one of them.

By now, even the most avid anti-predestination person should be seeing there might actually be some truth to it. "But wait; isn't it just speaking of us being predestined to be like Christ after death? Why would we bother having missionaries if God has already decided who He is going to save?"

While predestination is a very Biblical doctrine, missionary work is very important. There was a time when I was helping support missionaries in Japan, Germany, & Russia as well as donating to a missionary organization. I do feel there is a choice in the matter but I believe we have no choice but to make the one we make. I believe God lets us make the "choice" so that we will love Him more. At the time of my salvation, I didn't know this. I just knew I wanted to choose God and it was a great feeling but now, through growing and studying, I honestly feel I had no choice but to say yes. I am so thankful for this. To say that missionaries are the ones doing the saving is ridiculous! We like to think and say that we led someone to the Lord but technically we didn't do anything but obey God faithfully through our works. We can't change anybody's mind. If we are witnessing and something happens it is because God has spoken through you and softened the other person's heart. That is totally His doing.

God hardens hearts as well as softens them. However, we must be careful not to cross over the fine line and claim that God is actively making one sin. In the end, a man will act in accordance with his nature. By nature, we are all children of wrath. It is only by the grace of

God that we can be transformed into a new creature (2 Corinthians 5:17). If one is predestined for Heaven then there is no way he can choose to be rebellious and ignore God. He may do that for a time but in the end he will turn back to God. A saint cannot lose their salvation. If they were sincere at the time of conversion, it is final. If one never returns before they die then I doubt their claimed salvation to begin with. That would mean they obviously aren't one of God's predestined. Romans 9:20-24 makes it very clear that God can create us for whatever purpose He wants. It also makes clear that He created some to be vessels meant for destruction. We were tools made to be used by God to give Him glory. Out of His mercy and grace He chose to appoint some of us to be vessels of glory. There was no choice in any of that. You don't make a pot and then let the pot choose its purpose. The Maker made us for a purpose and we are not to question it even if that purpose is a vessel of destruction. Just because one goes through life living for themselves does not mean there is no way they are predestined. God could have already chosen this person but is letting them live their life making choices for themselves. In the end none of that will matter because if they were chosen by God before time began, that person WILL turn to Him and be saved. Just because they are predestined by God does not mean they are already saved. It just means that they will be before they die and there is no changing that fact.

R.C. Sproul

> God is not required to seek the sinner's permission for doing with the sinner what he pleases. The sinner didn't ask to be born in the country of his birth, to his parents, or even to be born at all. Nor did the sinner ask to be born with a fallen nature. All these things were determined by God's sovereign decision. If God does all this that affects the sinner's eternal destiny, what could possibly be wrong for him to go one more step to insure his salvation?....If it pleases God to save some and not all, there is nothing wrong with that. God is not under obligation to save anybody. If he chooses to save some, that in no way obligates him to save the rest....Let us assume that all men are guilty of sin in the sight of God. From that mass of guilty humanity, God sovereignly decides to give mercy to some of them. What do the rest get? They get justice. The saved get mercy and the

> unsaved get justice. Nobody gets injustice.[i]

Why do some have such a hard to accepting this? Maybe it's because we have a hard time seeing a loving, merciful God doing something like this? Maybe it's because we don't think it is fair? What about the righteous, just, God that He is? Have we forgotten about Him? Today's Christianity teaches all about the touchy, feely, loving, rewarding side of things and doesn't really touch on the rest. There are many facets to God. We can't forget this.

God gives us free will. We can either choose Him or choose against Him. Does this contradict everything I just stated? Not at all! If we already knew we were saved, we wouldn't really have to worry about much. It's like money. A kid from a poor family values what money he has and how he got it. A snotty rich kid couldn't care less. He has the money and he knows nobody can take it away from him. If we never made a choice to accept God do you honestly think we would cherish that gift as much as we do? Yes, God knows who will choose Him. He knows this because He has already chosen us. He lets us come to Him in our own time (which is actually His time). Yes, we choose to come to Him but it was going to happen regardless because He chose us. Of course, we had no idea that He chose us until after we accepted Him. One can spend their entire life thinking they were chosen by God and just to prove Him wrong will never accept Him. I can guarantee I know where that person will go when they die. It certainly won't be Heaven because it will turn out that they weren't chosen by God. When we make that choice to trust in Jesus it is something that nobody can explain. All of a sudden, you just know. Those who think they can outsmart God by refusing Him will never know.

R.C. Sproul

> We "feel" that we make real choices, and while our experience cannot be the final norm for our theology, neither can we deny its importance. We believe and feel that our choices are real because

> we have real wills with real inclinations, preferences, and so forth even as all that we decide is part of God's sovereign will.[ii]

At the same time, as Christians, we have a calling to witness to nonbelievers. Only God knows who He has called. We are not privy to this information. God has called us to be fishers of men (Matthew 4:19). Because of this calling, we have no excuse. We cannot use predestination as an excuse to not witness. Again, we do not know which fish will bite the hook. This does not change our responsibility.

Some have used Proverbs 3:5-6 to say that God does not intervene until one "acknowledges" Him. God knows our heart's desires. I honestly believe He takes our heart's desires into account in His plan. Before the beginning of time, He knew our heart's desires. From the moment we get saved our heart's desires mesh with God's desires. Our body's desires may differ but our heart's desires will always side with God if we are truly His. Yes, God has a plan. No, we can't change His plan. Yes, we should trust His plan. Yes, we can be thankful He has a plan for us. I would hate to think I was making blind choices in this world. I am comforted by the fact that God has a plan for me and that I am living it out. The biggest hurdle to get over is the fact that everyone wants to be in charge of their own life. We already know once we get saved, we give our lives to God. We always say that and we always ask God to guide us but we still want to keep control. What are we really asking for when we ask Him to guide us? Are we asking Him to give us advice so we can choose what advice to keep and what to ignore? It doesn't work that way. Like I stated before, God has a plan for us but He lets us make these "choices" so that we will value the outcome and His love. It's just that our choices coincide with His. Our timing coincides with His. If God wants me to sit in a chair at a given time, I can guarantee I will sit in that chair. If I decide to outsmart God by sitting in a different chair at that time then my heart is not really in God and I should re-evaluate my salvation. If I am truly with God then my desires will match His plan. If my desires do not match His plan, then my heart is not with Him and I am in big trouble. The funny part is that regardless of my desires, I still followed His plan by sitting in that chair. If I sat in chair # 2 then that was His plan all along but in my mind I have outsmarted God by being rebellious. We never know God's plan unless we desire to follow Him. If we are matching our hearts with God's then we know that everything we do is in His plan & His timing and we can take comfort in that.

Some make the claim that God foreknew those who would turn to Him. They say this is the actual meaning of Romans 9. This is based off of Romans 8:29. While it was quoted in our defense at the beginning of the chapter, many today actually use it in defense of free will.

Romans 8:29

> For those whom He foreknew, He also predestined to become conformed to the image of His Son, so that He would be the firstborn among many brethren;

While this might look like justification that God foreknew the decisions of everybody and chose the ones who would turn to Him, it is not accurate. Let's look at verses 29 and 30 together.

Romans 8:29-30

> For those whom He foreknew, He also predestined to become conformed to the image of His Son, so that He would be the firstborn among many brethren; and those whom He predestined, He also called; and these whom He called, He also justified; and these whom He justified, He also glorified.

According to this, God only foreknew a select group of individuals. Therefore, it stands to reason that anybody outside of this select group was not foreknown by God. That being said, this is not to say God is ignorant of anything. It means He knows us on a personal level (Jeremiah 1:5, Matthew 7:23, Galatians 4:9). I know my next door neighbor but not nearly on the personal level as I know my wife. My neighbor and I have knowledge of each other but my wife & I have a loving relationship WITH each other. What does this verse really say?

- God knew those whom He predestined to be conformed to the image of His Son.
- God called those whom He predestined.
- God justified those whom He called
- God glorified those whom He justified

God glorified, justified, called, and predestined those whom He knew ahead of time.

1 Corinthians 8:3

> But if anyone loves God, he is known by Him.

God knows those who love Him. In accordance with Romans 8:29-30, those who love God are also predestined by God. It does not say God foreknew who would choose Him, therefore predestining those select few as the Elect. It says God foreknew the Elect already. He predestined some to be conformed to the image of His Son and as a result, knows us personally on a loving level.

Furthermore, the word used in verse 29 for "predestined" is προορί/ζω (*proorizo*). This word does not imply knowledge in advance. It refers to limitations and ordinations. Verse 7 and 8 tell us, by our own nature, it is impossible to love God. It says we show hostility toward God so long as we are in our flesh and goes on to say how it is impossible to please God. I'd say so! How can one possibly please God while hating Him? If it is impossible to love God of our own choice, how much more impossible is it to claim that God predestined someone who hates Him based on their love for Him?

He foreknew those whom He predestined. As a result, we love Him. Yes, God did indeed foreknow who would choose Him and love Him. That is because it was He who predestined them to such a calling.

But doesn't God desire all men to be saved and come to repentance?

1 Timothy 2:4

> Who desires all men to be saved and to come to the knowledge of the truth.

It is very easy to confuse the Will of God versus the wants of God. God's Will is that His elect will be called to Him and that certain people will be vessels fitted unto glory while others are vessels fitted unto destruction. God hates sin yet it exists. If He hates sin, He obviously would desire that sin did not exist. The fact that it does exist tells us that God's desires sometimes sit on the back burner in order to accomplish His Will. God Wills that sin be punished. That is why Hell exists. Picture a father. His son does something wrong and needs a spanking as discipline. The father always says it is going to hurt him more than the child. The father desires not to spank his son but he also knows he has to in order to discipline or punish. It is the same idea only God is punishing some (for the sinful nature of man) while saving others (the Elect).

God does not Will that all have eternal life. If he Willed it, it would be so. God hates sin and it saddens Him but He is just and righteous. Christianity is not for the happy, feel good person. It is not meant to attract people. It is the Truth about a loving but righteous God that sent His son to die on the cross and rise again three days later so that His Elect will have a way to come to Him. It is about us worshiping that God and being thankful for His actions. It is about promised persecution but also the promise of a loving Father that will get us through anything.

Sin destroys everything. While it was our actions that caused us to fall away from God, this was all determined before the beginning of the foundation of the world. God knew that sin was going to happen. He knows everything. It was in the midst of this knowledge that He chose His Elect from among the sinners of the world. Again, it was before time began. Thankfully, God gave us a way to turn to Him through His Son. Once we "choose" Him, there is no turning back. We are one of the Elect and have finally, in God's timing, turned to Him. If a man truly believes in God AND repents, he is saved. One of the Elect cannot refuse God. On the same token, one of the non-elect can never choose God because it is impossible to seek Him. We do not seek God until He places the gift of faith in us.

2 Corinthians 5:17-19

> Therefore, if anyone is in Christ, he is a new creation; the old has gone, the new has come! All this is from God, who reconciled us to himself through Christ and gave us the ministry of reconciliation: that God was reconciling the world to himself in Christ, not counting men's sins against them. And he has committed to us the message of reconciliation.

The verse above says that we are new creations in Christ. God chose His Elect. He created some to vessels fitted for destruction and others to be vessels fitted for glory. Just because God chose us does not mean that we are in Him yet.

The Elect are still separated from God because of sin. It was through the death of Christ that the reconciliation occurred. Jesus made it possible to come to God. Once God places that gift of faith on us, our heart is changed. We are no longer spiritually dead. Now we see

God for who He is and our hearts are changed forever. Through the blood of Christ we are reconciled. The blood of Christ is not meant for all men. The vessels fitted for destruction will remain spiritually dead while the vessels fitted for glory will become new creations once the gift of faith is bestowed upon us and our heart is softened in God's own time.

Yes, He will accept any who come to Him in true repentance **BUT** that number is limited (*proorizo*) to the Elect. That is why God will accept them. It's because He has already chosen them. The Bible says that it is impossible to have a desire for Him because we are spiritually dead. The only ones that will have a desire for Him are the Elect who were chosen before the foundation of the world. This means that the Elect are already chosen. It hurts to think of it that way but that's what the Bible says about it. Some things in the Bible hurt but they are still true. The good news is that even someone who may seem lost may still be one of the Elect and just hasn't been called yet. Remain hopeful and keep spreading the doctrine of Christ.

Please do not confuse predestination with being a robot. There is definitely free will in our lives. Our free will just does not extend to our salvation. We can surely refuse to go preach and witness to others. This is an act of direct disobedience to God but we are still capable of doing it. Jonah did it. In the end he came around but he was reluctant to do so and was even angry. Regardless, he still made his own choices. We can do the same. We are called to go out and be fishers of men. This is a duty that God has assigned to us. He uses us in this manner. It is not us saving anyone with our words. We are simply showing the love of God and letting God speak through us. Only God knows His Elect. We are called to witness to everyone because God does not share with us who His Elect are. Do I believe that one of God's Elect will perish if we do not witness to them? Not at all! It is impossible for one of the Elect to go to Hell. I fully believe God will still bring this person to Himself in His own time but we will certainly take a hit due to our disobedience. Even if the hit is just a chance for Satan to tempt us while we are down, it is a hit nonetheless. In the end, it all brings glory to God.

---

[i] R.C. Sproul, Chosen By God [Ligonier Ministries, 2011] pg. 24-26

[ii] R.C. Sproul, Chosen By God [Ligonier Ministries, 2011] pg. 168

7 GIFTS OF THE SPIRIT

God has not left us to fend for ourselves. In every believer, He has bestowed a special gift. These gifts are known as the gifts of the Spirit. Each one is special in its own unique way. Despite this wonderful news, there is much controversy surrounding the gifts as we will soon see.

1 Corinthians 12:8-10

> For to one is given the word of wisdom through the Spirit, and to another the word of knowledge according to the same Spirit; to another faith by the same Spirit, and to another gifts of healing by the one Spirit, and to another the effecting of miracles, and to another prophecy, and to another the distinguishing of spirits, to another various kinds of tongues, and to another the interpretation of tongues.

While others are listed in Scripture, we will focus on the ones above. We can see that the gifts include:

1) word of wisdom

2) word of knowledge

3) faith

4) healing

5) miracles

6) prophecy

7) distinguishing of spirits

8) speaking tongues

9) interpretation of tongues

The truth is always important. In fact, John 8:32 tells us that the truth will set us free. It is my hope that by the end of this chapter, you will have a better understanding of these gifts as well as an understanding of the errors of many churches today in their private interpretation of the gifts.

1 Corinthians 12:4 & 11

> Now there are varieties of gifts, but the same Spirit.........But one and the same Spirit works all these things, distributing to each one individually just as He wills.

The gifts are not something that we pick and choose. They are given by God and God alone. He has a plan and He gives each gift as He wills. We are to seek out what it is that He has given to us so that we can better serve Him but we are not to seek out specific gifts in hope that He will bless us with them at a later date. We are given our gifts at the moment of salvation.

1 Corinthians 12:8a

> For to one is given the **word of wisdom** through the Spirit,

The Greek word used for "word" is *logos*. It refers to a speaking ability. The Greek word used for "wisdom" is *Sophia*. It refers to the ability to put God's Word into practical use. Pastors, counselors, & encouragers are all people who would probably possess the gift of wisdom as they all speak practical advice from Scripture to others.

1 Corinthians 12:8b

> and to another the **word of knowledge** according to the same Spirit;

Once again, I can see the word *logos* being used. Because of this, we know that the gift of knowledge is another speaking gift.

1 Corinthians 2:14

> But a natural man does not accept the things of the Spirit of God, for they are foolishness to him; and he cannot understand them, because they are spiritually appraised.

Only one led by the Spirit can understand the things of the Spirit. While this is true of all believers, some have been gifted with the ability to dive in deep, exegetically extract the knowledge of Scripture, and relay it to others. This is a gift of teachers. We can also safely say one who has the gift of a word of wisdom also has the gift of a word of knowledge as one must know the Word of God before they can speak of it. The two are very similar yet quite different. The gift of a word of knowledge is the ability to relay the knowledge in a spoken manner while the gift of a word of wisdom is the ability to apply it practically in day to day use while also instructing others how to do so.

1 Corinthians 12:9a

> to another **faith** by the same Spirit,

This gift of faith is not the same as the faith that brings salvation. Every believer has the latter gift while the former is given to certain believers as God desires.

Ephesians 2:8

> For by grace you have been saved through faith; and that not of yourselves, it is the gift of God;

Saving faith is indeed a gift. Do not be mistaken. The only reason we are saved is because God, in His grace, gifted us with saving faith. Despite this truth, this is not what Paul is speaking of in verse 9. The spiritual gift of faith is the ability to consistently trust the power and promises of God in an extraordinary encouraging way.

1 Corinthians 13:2b

> and if I have all faith, so as to remove mountains, but do not have love, I am nothing.

Matthew 17:20

> And He said to them, "Because of the littleness of your faith; for truly I say to you, if you have faith the size of a mustard seed, you will say to this mountain, 'Move from here to there,' and it will move; and nothing will be impossible to you.

We can see a differentiation. Saving faith is our belief in Christ which is granted us in the Spirit. The spiritual gift of faith being referred to above is one who trusts in the power of God through prayer. It is one who trusts in the goodness of God in times of adversity. It is one who trusts in the sovereignty of God in times of confusion.

Matthew 16:8

> But Jesus, aware of this, said, "You men of little faith, why do you discuss among yourselves that you have no bread?

This seems to imply that there are varying degrees of faith. While all believers have the fullness of saving faith, some have more faith than others regarding trusting the promises of God. Those with the spiritual gift of faith will be a step above the others in this area. This is not something to brag about but rather, something to put into practice to edify the Church. This person, through their trust in God, can encourage other believers through their actions. In their steadfastness, they can encourage others to stand firm. In their calmness, they can encourage others to cast their anxiety on God. They can be a living example of Philippians 4:13.

Philippians 4:13

> I can do all things through Him who strengthens me.

I believe the apostles had the gift of faith as did all the other martyrs throughout history. It takes a lot of faith to stand up for God in the face of death and speak unashamed that Jesus Christ is Lord.

1 Corinthians 12:9b

> and to another gifts of **healing** by the one Spirit,

The spiritual gift of healing is the ability to fully heal someone. This is not the same as doctors. Doctors heal through modern medicine as well as the study of the body. Those who were gifted with healing simply said it and it was so. There were no chants, incantations, or spells. It did not involve hours of surgery or uncontrollable bleeding. Just as creation came to be by God simply willing it to be so, the spiritual gift of healing would fully heal instantaneously at the will of the one possessing it.

Matthew 10:1

> Jesus summoned His twelve disciples and gave them authority over unclean spirits, to cast them out, and to heal every kind of disease and every kind of sickness.

Acts 8:5-7

> Philip went down to the city of Samaria and began proclaiming Christ to them. The crowds with one accord were giving attention to what was said by Philip, as they heard and saw the signs which he was performing. For in the case of many who had unclean spirits, they were coming out of them shouting with a loud voice; and many who had been paralyzed and lame were healed.

Matthew 8:16-17

> When evening came, they brought to Him many who were demon-possessed; and He cast out the spirits with a word, and healed all who were ill. This was to fulfill what was spoken through Isaiah the prophet: "HE HIMSELF TOOK OUR INFIRMITIES AND CARRIED AWAY OUR DISEASES."

It did not partially heal only to have the illness come back within a few days. It was not restricted to those with improvable ailments. It was not a measure of faith in the recipient of the healing. It was authority within an individual believer to heal **every** kind of disease and sickness including death. Notice what it says in Matthew 8:17.

Matthew 8:17

> This was to fulfill what was spoken through Isaiah the prophet: "HE HIMSELF TOOK OUR INFIRMITIES AND CARRIED AWAY OUR DISEASES."

The very purpose of the gift of healing was in order to fulfill Scripture. While the previous gifts are all permanent gifts, there were some gifts that were temporary. This is one of the four that we are going to discuss which are commonly referred to as the "sign gifts." The gift of healing was meant to be a sign. Jews saw Gentiles as being a lower class that God would never look kindly upon. Jesus commonly taught of the Gentiles being grafted into the vine. Salvation was no longer limited to Jews only. Imagine the response when they saw Gentiles being healed in the ways described in the above verses. These "lesser quality" people were receiving the power and blessing of God; something that was previously reserved for the Jews. The blind could see. The paralyzed could walk. The dead were brought back to life. All of these things were done to authenticate the message of the apostles. Today, the Word of God has already been authenticated. The Spiritual gift of healing is no longer necessary. We are no longer in the transition period from the old covenant to the new covenant. We are no longer given the gift of healing as its purpose has been fulfilled. God may still heal if He chooses to do so but that power is no longer gifted to believers to perform in and of themselves.

1 Corinthians 12:10a

> and to another the effecting of **miracles**,

This is another one of the temporary gifts. The gift of miracles was not meant for boasting nor was it meant to edify the Church. They were meant to authenticate the apostolic message just as healing did.

John 20:30-31

> Therefore many other signs Jesus also performed in the presence of the disciples, which are not written in this book; but these have been written **so that you may believe that Jesus is the Christ**, the Son of God; and that believing you may have life in His name.

Even the miracles and signs produced by Jesus were not for the purpose of showing off or personal gain. They were produced in order to authenticate the apostolic message and confirm the name of Christ.

2 Corinthians 12:12

> The signs of a true apostle were performed among you with all perseverance, by signs and wonders and miracles.

Hebrews 2:3b-4a

> After it was at the first spoken through the Lord, it was confirmed to us by those who heard, God also testifying with them, both by signs and wonders and by various miracles

The gift of miracles had a purpose of confirmation. It confirmed the authenticity of the apostles. It confirmed the authenticity of Christ. Today, we have God's complete Word with full authority. We no longer need the confirmation because we are out of the transitional period. Because of this, the gift of miracles has ceased to exist. It fulfilled its purpose.

B.B. Warfield

> These miraculous gifts were part of the credentials of the apostles, as authoritative agents of God in founding the church. Their function confined them distinctly to the apostolic church, and they necessarily passed away with it.[i]

1 Corinthians 12:10b

> and to another **prophecy**,

Prophecy is one that has been cause for much confusion over the years as well. We think of a prophet as being a man who can tell the future. While this was often the case in the Old Testament, this is not the case today. Prophecy is **not** one of the temporary gifts. It is a permanent gift of God that He continues to give today. However, it is a very different office today.

The Greek word used for prophecy is *propheteia*. It simply means to speak forth or to proclaim the truth of God. There were indeed many times in the Old Testament where God used prophets to speak newly revealed truth that had previously been concealed. This was divine revelation. However, this was not the primary purpose of the gift. The primary purpose of prophecy was to speak forth publicly of God in a profound manner. Sometimes it was new revelation while other times, they only reassured people of truth that was already revealed previously.

Revelation 22:18

> I testify to everyone who hears the words of the prophecy of this book: if anyone adds to them, God will add to him the plagues which are written in this book;

We have God's complete revelation. It ended with the revelation of John in the book of Revelation. If one claims to have a newly revealed Word of God, it **must** be recorded and added to Scripture just like every other bit of prophetic words were added. God's revelation is not meant for just a specific area of believers. His Word is applicable to all believers everywhere and He made it available to us all in Scripture.

No one is to add to Scripture. His divine revelation has ended and is complete within Scripture.

Remember that we spoke of the gifts of knowledge and wisdom going hand in hand. Both of those gifts accompany the modern day gift of prophecy. Today, one with the gift of prophecy is able to know and share God's revealed word through the gift of knowledge while also being able to apply it through the gift of wisdom.

Revelation 19:10b

> For the testimony of Jesus is the spirit of prophecy.

John 5:39

> You search the Scriptures because you think that in them you have eternal life; it is these that testify about Me;

1 Corinthians 14:37

> If anyone thinks he is a prophet or spiritual, let him recognize that the things which I write to you are the Lord's commandment.

The spirit of prophecy is to testify of Jesus. That testimony is found in Scripture. If one claims to be a prophet, he needs to teach from Scripture and proclaim the testimony of Jesus found within. He is not to add to Scripture by proclaiming a new word but is to speak forth the already written word through his special gift.

1 Corinthians 12:10c

> and to another the **distinguishing of spirits**,

This is a very special gift in a day of deception. It is the unique ability to be able to tell the difference between the authentic and the counterfeit.

John 8:44

> You are of your father the devil, and you want to do the desires of your father. He was a murderer from the beginning, and does not stand in the truth because there is no truth in him. Whenever he speaks a lie, he speaks from his own nature, for he is a liar and the father of lies.

Satan is a liar. He is the father of lies. He does his hardest to twist the Word of God and lead people astray. He often takes sound doctrine and adds a slight twist to it so that it is believable enough but still false enough that people will go away from the Truth. We can see this happening in modern medicine where people turn to pills for joy instead of the Spirit because they have bought into the belief that it is necessary. We see it in schools where people believe God should remain off campus so we accept it as normal. The most believable lie is a half-truth and Satan has an unlimited supply of these in his arsenal.

1 John 4:1

> Beloved, do not believe every spirit, but test the spirits to see whether they are from God, because many false prophets have gone out into the world.

This is something that we are all called to do as believers in Christ. We should all be searching the Scriptures. However, one with the gift of the distinguishing of spirits has a built in alarm system so to speak. They hear something false and it sounds the bells and whistles. I often feel this way when I hear people speak. Something just sounds off about it and it prompts to me either speak out or to search the

Scriptures myself. More often than not, I find that indeed the person was taking it out of context or was speaking a lie. One with the gift of discernment will often be the first or only one to recognize a false teaching though those around him see nothing wrong with it.

1 Corinthians 12:10d

> to another various kinds of **tongues**, and to another the **interpretation of tongues**.

Tongues is the most controversial gift out of them all. Many people believe it has continued into the present day (Continuationists) while many others believe they ceased upon the completion of God's Word (Cessationists). I fall into the latter category in the belief that they have ceased. Before we can get into whether or not they still exist, we first need to look at their purpose.

1 Corinthians 14:22a

> So then tongues are for a sign, not to those who believe but to unbelievers;

That sign is clarified in Isaiah 28. The whole purpose of tongues was as a sign of judgment to unbelieving Israel during the transition period of old to new covenant when the Gentiles were being grafted in. As we covered, it was seen as outlandish that a Gentile would possess anything of God. After all, the Jews were God's chosen people. This sign of judgment from Isaiah 28 is quoted in 1 Corinthians 14:21.

1 Corinthians 14:21

> BY MEN OF STRANGE TONGUES AND BY THE LIPS OF STRANGERS I WILL SPEAK TO THIS PEOPLE, AND EVEN SO THEY WILL NOT

> LISTEN TO ME

Tongues were always real languages. Had it been gibberish, the Gentiles would have looked insane. This would not have been a sign of judgment on Israel as they would have looked at the Gentiles as being lower than they already viewed them. They were real languages that authenticated the work of God in them.

Acts 10:45-46a

> All the circumcised believers who came with Peter were amazed, because the gift of the Holy Spirit had been poured out on the Gentiles also. For they were hearing them speaking with tongues and exalting God.

Acts 2:6-8

> And when this sound occurred, the crowds came together, and were bewildered because each one of them was hearing them speak in his own language. They were amazed and astonished, saying, "Why, are not all these who are speaking Galileans? And how is it that we each hear them in our own language to which we were born?

I already stated in 1 Corinthians 14:22 how it says tongues are a sign not to those who believe but to unbelievers. Keep this in mind.

1 Corinthians 14:2

> For one who speaks in a tongue does not speak to men but to God; for no one understands, but in his spirit he speaks mysteries.

1 Corinthians 14:4

> One who speaks in a tongue edifies himself; but one who prophesies edifies the church.

This is not a praise directing people to speak to God in a private prayer language as is the argument of most every Charismatic I have ever spoken with. It is the exact opposite. First of all, we see Paul is telling of the greatness of prophecy because it edifies the Church. Tongues were not meant to do this. Tongues were not even primarily for the believer. They were for the unbeliever's benefit. If tongues were meant to be a prayer language, why would Paul so boldly state that they are not for the believer? As with the other temporary sign gifts, the gift of tongues was meant to authenticate the apostolic word.

Furthermore, let's go back to verse 2. It says that one who speaks in a tongue does not speak to men but to God. Many Charismatics take this to mean they can pray to God in a private prayer language that is not meant for men. However, further examination of the text refutes this theory.

It clearly says the man who does this speaks mysteries. He speaks things he does not understand. In a sense, it amounts to futile babbling that he only hopes is making it to God in some cohesive manner on the other end. Also notice that the spirit it speaks of is not the Holy Spirit but rather, the spirit of the man.

Charismatics make the claim that the private prayer language is meant for self edification and not for others. In verse 22, quoted previously, Paul says tongues are not meant for the believer. This is strike 1. Furthermore, we know that tongues need to be understood in order to have any edifying effect whatsoever. Verse 2 does say that tongues edifies oneself while prophecy edifies the Church. However, Paul was being sarcastic here. We see sarcasm being used all throughout this epistle such as 4:8-10 and 14:16. The Corinthians desired the "wow" gifts for selfish reasons. There was a sense of satisfaction in them knowing that they had what they thought to be the greater gifts that everyone could see. He was pointing out their selfishness. There was no actual edifying going on. They just had a sense of self satisfaction in their "achievements."

1 Corinthians 14:6

> But now, brethren, if I come to you speaking in tongues, what will I profit you unless I speak to you either by way of revelation or of knowledge or of prophecy or of teaching?

Unless there was interpretation, there was no profit. If there is no profit, there is no edification. If there is no edification, there is no point.

1 Corinthians 14:12

> So also you, since you are zealous of spiritual gifts, seek to abound for the edification of the church.

The Corinthians desired gifts that could astonish. Paul was instructing them to take this zeal and apply it to the edification of the Church instead of toward selfish desires that are not of the Spirit.

1 Corinthians 14:14-15

> For if I pray in a tongue, my spirit prays, but my mind is unfruitful. What is the outcome then? I will pray with the spirit and I will pray with the mind also; I will sing with the spirit and I will sing with the mind also.

Paul is saying that to pray in tongues as a private prayer language (as they were apparently doing even back then) is in vain. Paul goes so far as to say it is unfruitful. If there is no fruit, there can certainly be no edification. Paul doesn't just leave it as being unfruitful for the Church as he differentiates in other passages. He plainly says it is unfruitful period. Unless the one speaking can understand it, there is no fruit. This is because his mind is unfruitful. I've actually heard Charismatics claim that freeing the mind is the goal. Paul says the exact opposite. He does not continue by saying to let your mind run free and pray an unknown tongue to God hoping that He will understand it and edify you. Paul says instead he will pray not only with the spirit but also with the mind. One can only pray with the mind if he understands what he is praying.

1 Corinthians 14:13

> Therefore let one who speaks in a tongue pray that he may interpret.

Notice it does not say pray that someone else can interpret. It says for the speaker to pray that he can interpret. This was more sarcasm. Paul knew they were speaking gibberish and he challenged them. If they weren't going to stop, at least pray that they can interpret their own nonsense.

1 Corinthians 14:28

> but if there is no interpreter, he must keep silent in the church; and let him speak to himself and to God.

This is another one used by Charismatics to claim they can pray to God in an unknown private prayer language. I have already given more than enough evidence that there is no such thing as a private prayer language because it is unfruitful, unprofitable, and has no edifying value whatsoever. In turn, the praying to God mentioned in verse 28 can only mean in their own language. If they felt compelled to speak in tongues but there was no interpreter, instead let that man remain quiet and pray to God with value in his own language.

1 Corinthians 12:3

> Therefore I make known to you that no one speaking by the Spirit of God says, "Jesus is accursed";

Many Charismatics say that they have experienced it so it can't be false. Well, the above verse should refute this in full. Apparently, some were claiming to speak in the Spirit yet they were saying, "Jesus is accursed." In the same manner, just because someone has claimed to experience the gift of tongues does not mean it is valid if it is outside of the framework of Scripture and goes against the very rebukes of Paul.

1 Corinthians 13:8

> Love never fails; but if there are gifts of prophecy, they will be done away; if there are tongues, they will cease; if there is knowledge, it will be done away.

Upon first glance, it appears that prophecy, tongues, and knowledge will all cease together at some point. However, further study shows different timelines. The Greek word used for cease is *pauo*. It means to simply cease to exist or to run out much like a battery that loses charge. It just dies off. The Greek word used for done away is *katargeo*. It implies an external force putting a stop to something. It sets tongues apart from the rest. It says prophecy and knowledge will be done away but tongues will cease.

1 Corinthians 13:9-10

> For we know in part and we prophesy in part; but when the perfect comes, the partial will be done away.

Here we can see knowledge and prophesy being together again. However, notice that no reference to tongues can be found. Let's look at it again.

1 Corinthians 13:8-10

> Love never fails; but if there are gifts of prophecy, they will be done away; if there are tongues, they will cease; if there is knowledge, it will be done away. For we know in part and we prophesy in part; but when the perfect comes, the partial will be done away.

The gifts of knowledge and prophecy will be done away with the coming of the perfect; however, tongues is not mentioned because it will have already ceased to exist beforehand. Some say since it does not list the other gifts, we can't come to this conclusion. However, it was speaking of all three (prophecy, knowledge, and tongues). It mentions all three of them, differentiates the way tongues will go, and then mentions the two that will still be around.

I do not believe the perfect is the completion of Scripture as things are still far from perfect. I do not believe the perfect is the coming of Christ for the same reason. I believe the perfect to be when I get to Heaven. Only at this point will all things be perfect. Until then, the gifts of knowledge and prophecy will remain. We know the gift of tongues will have ceased to exist sometime before then. It is a matter of figuring out if that time has already come or if it will come sometime in the future. I hope I have given enough Scripture references to show how it is over and how the sign of judgment has already been delivered.

O. Palmer Robertson

> Tongues served well to show that Christianity, though begun in the cradle of Judaism, was not to be distinctively Jewish...Now that the transition [between Old and New Covenants] has been made, the sign of transition has no abiding value in the life of the church.
>
> Today there is no need for a sign to show that God is moving from the single nation of Israel to all the nations. That movement has become an accomplished fact. As in the case of the founding office of apostle, so the particularly transitional gift of tongues has fulfilled its function as covenantal sign for the Old and New Covenant people of God. Once having fulfilled that role, it has no further function among the people of God.[ii]

Regarding the signs gifts being temporary, Scripture itself attests to it.

Hebrews 2:3b-4a

> After it was at the first spoken through the Lord, it **was confirmed** to us by those who heard, God also testifying with them, both by signs and wonders and by various miracles

2 Corinthians 12:12

> The signs of a true apostle **were** **performed** among you with all perseverance, by signs and wonders and miracles.

We covered earlier that the sign gifts were meant to authenticate apostolic teaching. These verses seem to indicate that the sign gifts had already faded away. It is as if he is telling a story of the past to tap their memories and keep them going strong. They **had been** shown. It **had been** confirmed. It was not a current ongoing confirmation by signs and wonders but rather a past tense instance of something that had already taken place and was no longer.

Thomas R. Edgar

> Since these gifts and signs did cease, the burden of proof is entirely on the charismatics to prove their validity. Too long Christians have assumed that the noncharismatic must produce incontestable Biblical evidence that the miraculous sign gifts did cease. However, noncharismatics have no burden to prove this, since it has already been proved by history. It is irrefutable fact admitted by many Pentecostals. Therefore the charismatics must prove Biblically that the sign gifts will start up again during the Church Age and that today's phenomena are this reoccurrence. In other words they must prove that their experiences are the reoccurrence of gifts that have not occurred for almost 1,900 years.[iii]

If you ever get into a discussion of the sign gifts with a Charismatic, you will doubtlessly hear the question, "But have you ever experienced them?" or perhaps the statement, "You can't comment on something you have never experienced." As we covered earlier, we are all called to prove all things through Scripture. If this can't be done, we are to reject the experience as invalid. God will never give us something that is outside of Scripture but Satan just might throw a twisted half-truth our way. Be diligent in your study of the Word and ask God to show you what He has gifted you with so that you may edify the Church.

[i] John MacArthur, The MacArthur New Testament Commentary on First Corinthians [Moody Publishers, 1984] pg. 302

[ii] O. Palmer Robertson, "Tongues: Sign of Covenantal Curse and Blessing," The Westminster Theological Journal 38 (Fall 1975 – Spring 1976), pg 53

[iii] Thomas R. Edgar, The Cessation of the Sign Gifts, [Bibliotheca Sacra, October-December 1988], pg. 374

8 GIFTS TO EDIFY

In the last chapter, we spoke on the gifts of the Spirit. We learned what each gift was designed for. We learned that there were temporary gifts meant for authentication as well as permanent gifts meant for edification. In this chapter, we are going to focus on the importance of edification and how the gifts interact.

Romans 15:1-2

> Now we who are strong ought to bear the weaknesses of those without strength and not just please ourselves. Each of us is to please his neighbor for his good, to his **edification**.

The Greek word used for edification is *oikodomeo*. It literally means to build up or to erect. The verse above is telling us that we are to help build up others and not just please ourselves. It implies a selfless act of love. In fact, the connotation of the above verse even implies a sacrificial act.

1 Corinthians 12:6-11

> There are varieties of effects, but the same God who works all things in all persons. But to each one is given the manifestation of the

> Spirit for the common good. For to one is given the word of wisdom through the Spirit, and to another the word of knowledge according to the same Spirit; to another faith by the same Spirit, and to another gifts of healing by the one Spirit, and to another the effecting of miracles, and to another prophecy, and to another the distinguishing of spirits, to another various kinds of tongues, and to another the interpretation of tongues. But one and the same Spirit works all these things, distributing to each one individually just as He wills.

First, let's recap the nine temporary and permanent gifts.

Temporary (4)

10) healing

11) miracles

12) tongues

13) interpretation of tongues

Permanent (5)

1) word of wisdom

2) word of knowledge

3) prophecy

4) distinguishing of spirits

5) faith

Healing, miracles, and tongues were all used to authenticate the apostolic message. We saw they were limited in many ways and were even spoken of in the past tense of the later-written epistles as if they had already ceased to exist. However, we also saw the permanent gifts seemed to have a very different purpose. While the temporary sign gifts were for the unbelievers benefit, the permanent gifts seem to have a further reach within the Church.

Ephesians 4:11-12

> And He gave some as apostles, and some as prophets, and some as evangelists, and some as pastors and teachers, for the equipping of the saints for the work of service, to **the building up of the body of Christ**;

What good is a building if its walls are falling down? Structural integrity and support are vital to a building's strength and longevity. We can see the primary purpose of Spiritual gifts is for building up the body of Christ. They are for the edification, the *oikodomeo* of the body of Christ.

I spent a great deal of the last chapter speaking on tongues and helping to explain how their use was as a temporary sign gift toward unbelievers. The claim made by many Charismatics is that tongues is a private prayer language that is to be sought after. One of the verses they use to make this claim is 1 Corinthians 13:1a.

1 Corinthians 13:1a

> If I speak with the tongues of men and of angels

The claim is that Scripture clearly states there is a special language of angels that we can speak in. Some have made the claim that this is not only a private prayer language but possibly even the very basis of tongues. I showed in the previous chapter how every instance of tongues in Scripture was a known language. This alone should rule out the theory of angelic languages. Furthermore, every instance in Scripture of an angel speaking was in the native tongue of the people in whom they were speaking to. To top it all off, the surrounding verses in 1 Corinthians 13 paint a very different picture.

1 Corinthians 13:1-3

> If I speak with the tongues of men and of angels, but do not have love, I have become a noisy gong or a clanging cymbal. If I have the gift of prophecy, and know all mysteries and all knowledge; and if I have all faith, so as to remove mountains, but do not have love, I am nothing. And if I give all my possessions to feed the poor, and if I surrender my body to be burned, but do not have love, it profits me nothing.

Paul knew there was no way to know all the mysteries of God or have all knowledge. This is why he wrote, "we know in part and we prophesy in part." Despite this, he still wrote about knowing all mysteries and having all knowledge as an option. He writes of moving mountains with faith. While this one may seem legit since he is referencing a quote by Jesus, further study of the text in Matthew 17:20 shows that it was not literally saying a mountain would move. Jesus was using those words to make a point. It is also safe to assume Paul would not really give all he had to the poor as he needed things to survive on his own. He traveled a lot. Same goes for him offering his body to be burned. That is an absurd thought. Paul was using hyperbole to make a point. If every other point Paul is bringing up is clearly hyperbole, doesn't it stand to reason that the tongues of angels is hyperbole as well? To throw one real thing among a list of exaggerated points doesn't make any sense. The reason it doesn't make any sense is because this is not the case. Paul is not condoning speaking in an angelic tongue. In fact, he is doing the exact opposite.

The Corinthians were selfish. They loved showing off. They desired the sign gifts so that they could show off to one another. This is evident by Paul's writing to them.

1 Corinthians 12:11, 18-22 & 30-31

> But one and the same Spirit works all these things, distributing to each one individually just as He wills………But now God has placed

> the members, each one of them, in the body, just as He desired. If they were all one member, where would the body be? But now there are many members, but one body. And the eye cannot say to the hand, "I have no need of you"; or again the head to the feet, "I have no need of you." On the contrary, it is much truer that the members of the body which seem to be weaker are necessary;......... All do not have gifts of healings, do they? All do not speak with tongues, do they? All do not interpret, do they? But earnestly desire the greater gifts. And I show you a still more excellent way.

It is no secret that the Corinthians were seeking sign gifts. They thought highly of the sign gifts because they were visible. They thought less of the other gifts because they appeared to be less honorable. However, Paul tells them to seek the greater gifts. This says two things. One, the sign gifts were not the better gifts after all. Two, God grants them as He pleases so seeking after them is futile. Paul telling them to seek the greater gifts was yet another form of sarcasm that you can find all throughout his epistle. His point was not for the people of Corinth to seek gifts but rather, to accept what God has already blessed them with because they all have a purpose in the kingdom of God.

Ephesians 4:29

> Let no unwholesome word proceed from your mouth, but only such a word as is good for edification according to the need of the moment, so that it will give grace to those who hear.

Paul spends much time speaking against the misuse and counterfeiting of the sign gifts that was taking place. However, his primary goal is not to belittle the Corinthians but to build them up. This is why he spoke so much on love and edification. The Corinthians were lacking greatly in this area. They had selfish desires, sought after attention, mixed pagan beliefs into their faith, and thought less of any gift that appeared to be less honorable.

1 Corinthians 14:26

> What is the outcome then, brethren? When you assemble, each one has a psalm, has a teaching, has a revelation, has a tongue, has an interpretation. Let all things be done for edification.

If we continued to read, we would see Paul lays out the proper guidance for tongues. Remember, at the time 1 Corinthians was written, tongues was still an active gift. The problem was not the use but rather the misuse and even counterfeiting of this gift in the Corinthian church. In their services, they were all speaking at once, all speaking different things, and not interpreting any of it. It was utter chaos. There was no edification. This is why Paul says, "Let all things be done for edification."

In chapter 4, we covered legalism vs. licentiousness regarding meat sacrificed to idols. Strong Christians knew that it was perfectly fine to eat this meat as the idols had no power because they were false gods. However, newer Christians would see this and, because they had just gotten out of these pagan practices, thought it was sinful to eat the meat.

1 Corinthians 8:1 & 7-13

> Now concerning things sacrificed to idols, we know that we all have knowledge. Knowledge makes arrogant, but love edifies..........However not all men have this knowledge; but some, being accustomed to the idol until now, eat food as if it were sacrificed to an idol; and their conscience being weak is defiled. But food will not commend us to God; we are neither the worse if we do not eat, nor the better if we do eat. But take care that this liberty of yours does not somehow become a stumbling block to the weak. For if someone sees you, who have knowledge, dining in an idol's temple, will not his conscience, if he is weak, be strengthened to eat things sacrificed to idols? For through your knowledge he who is weak is ruined, the brother for whose sake Christ died. And so, by sinning against the brethren and wounding their conscience when it is weak, you sin against Christ. Therefore, if food causes my brother to stumble, I will never eat meat again, so that I will not cause my

> brother to stumble.

1 Corinthians 10:23

> All things are lawful, but not all things are profitable. All things are lawful, but not all things edify.

Edification is key. There are many things we have liberty to enjoy in Christ. However, there are a few things that we should take into account.

1) Will it cause another to stumble?
2) Will it distract from our focus on God?
3) Will it edify another?

If we are tearing down others at their own expense while building ourselves up using Christ as a covering, we are wrong. All things are lawful but not all things are profitable. All things are lawful but not all things edify.

Romans 14:19

> So then we pursue the things which make for peace and the building up of one another.

1 Corinthians 10:24

> Let no one seek his own good, but that of his neighbor.

The only way to properly build up one another is in love. When Paul ends chapter 12 with, "And I show you a still more excellent way" it is love that he is speaking of.

1 Corinthians 13:4-8 & 13

> Love is patient, love is kind and is not jealous; love does not brag and is not arrogant, does not act unbecomingly; it does not seek its own, is not provoked, does not take into account a wrong suffered, does not rejoice in unrighteousness, but rejoices with the truth; bears all things, believes all things, hopes all things, endures all things. Love never fails;………But now faith, hope, love, abide these three; but the greatest of these is love.

In English, we are very limited as we only have one word for love whereas the ancient Greek has four.

1) **Agape** – selfless, sacrificial, caring, enacted
2) **Eros** – romantic or sexual
3) **Philia** – close friendship or brotherly love
4) **Storge** – affection of family (i.e. parents toward their children)

The Greek word used in the passage above is agape. We rarely practice agape love. It just isn't in our nature to do so. We often feel philia, eros, or storge but agape normally isn't in the picture. This alone is the answer to many of our problems. We often hear 1 Corinthians 13 read at weddings. It is referred to as the Love Chapter. Unfortunately, most brides and grooms at the altar have no idea what it is they are really pledging to one another.

John 13:34

> A new commandment I give to you, that you love one another, even as I have loved you, that you also love one another.

In all things, practice agape love toward one another. It is not just saying the words but requires acting it out. Do not seek gifts that you wish you possessed. Instead, seek the gifts God has already blessed you with so that you can better serve His church. In all things seek to edify as this is agape love enacted.

9 JESUS IN HELL

How many of you jumped straight to this chapter checking to see if the Table of Contents had a typo? It's okay. You can admit it. Yes, you read it right. While it may sound blasphemous to one without understanding, by the end of this chapter, it may actually sound like solid doctrine.

We always say that God loved us so much that he gave His son to die on the cross but how many of us really stop to think about it? We all know Jesus died and rose again three days later but most people don't really think about the time in between.

Apostle's Creed

> I believe in God, the Father Almighty,
>   the Maker of heaven and earth,
>   and in Jesus Christ, His only Son, our Lord:
>
> Who was conceived by the Holy Ghost,
>   born of the virgin Mary,
>   suffered under Pontius Pilate,
>   was crucified, dead, and buried;
>
> **He descended into hell.**

> The third day He arose again from the dead;
>
> He ascended into heaven,
>   and sitteth on the right hand of God the Father Almighty;
>   from thence he shall come to judge the quick and the dead.
>
> I believe in the Holy Ghost;
>   the holy catholic church;
>   the communion of saints;
>   the forgiveness of sins;
>   the resurrection of the body;
>   and the life everlasting.
>
> Amen.

Not only did God send His son to die on the cross but He also sent His son to Hell for three days. Now, I want to clarify when I say Hell. I am not referring to a place of torment that we know it as. In English, we are very limited in our wording as we covered in chapter 8 regarding our one word for love versus the four words in ancient Greek. When I say Hell, I am actually referring to Hades, the Greek abode of the dead. I am merely referring to it as "Hell" for familiarities sake as this is what the vast majority know it as. Please keep this in mind as you see the many references to Hell in this chapter. As a whole, Hades did not refer to a place of suffering nor did it refer to a place of peace. It was simply the storage location, or abode, of the dead.

Despite having never sinned, Jesus was viewed as having the sin of the world on him. Obviously, he would not be able to enter into Heaven while viewed in this state by the Father. In fact, at this point, no human was in Heaven yet as the only way in is through the Son (John 14:6). The only other place for him to have gone during those three days was Hell. Imagine how happy Satan must've felt when he thought he had triumphed only to be proven wrong a few days later. Ever wonder what Jesus went through during those three days? Really stop to think about it. God loves us beyond our comprehension!

Some may ask why God would send His only begotten Son to Hell for even one day let alone three. I'm not one to guess why God set up the timeline the way He did but I am willing to bet the three days wasn't meant to "work off" any sin as if he were in some form of purgatory.

Hebrews 9:27-28

> And inasmuch as it is appointed for men to die once and after this comes judgment, so Christ also, having been offered once to bear the sins of many, will appear a second time for salvation without reference to sin, to those who eagerly await Him.

Jesus bore the sins of the entire world. He was condemned as guilty and unsanctified despite having committed no crime. Though never becoming a sinner, his innocence was imputed to us while, at the same time, our guilt and shame was imputed to him. Sin must be punished. Due to God being just, He issues no waivers. Sin will, and must, be dealt with according to His standard set forth from eternity. Our debt could not be brushed to the side. Jesus did more than declare us innocent. He transferred his innocence upon us while, simultaneously, transferring our guilt upon him. Because of this, He died and went to Hell. God's timeline said three days later he would rise. I don't know why He picked 3 days but He did and that's that. Jesus' judgment was Hell just as any others would have been. God had His plan for Jesus to rise. After he had risen, he was no longer filthy with sin. He had already died and received judgment. Jesus was alive for the second time. It was an entirely new life. It was a life that would never again see the sting of death.

Hebrews 9:27

> And inasmuch as it is appointed for men to die once and after this comes judgment,

As it is appointed unto man **once** to die. Jesus had defeated death, risen from the grave, and visited his disciples one last time before rejoining his Father in Heaven. I say rejoined because he was there since the beginning (Genesis 1:26).

To understand why Jesus went to Hell, we must understand the reasons people go to Hell:

1) They do not trust in Christ as their savior. They do not believe that he was the Son of God that died on the cross for our sins and rose again on the third day.
2) They cannot enter Heaven blemished with sin.
3) They have not asked Jesus to be the ultimate sacrifice for them and cover their sin as it happens.

A friend once attempted to prove this wrong by saying it was the blood of Christ that washes away our sins. In and of itself, this is correct theology. The point he was trying to make was that since Christ had already shed his blood, he no longer had a need to go to Hell because his blood covered it all while he was still on the cross. The same argument was used for the thief on the cross. The problem with this is that the new covenant wasn't established until Jesus had risen from the dead. The thief on the cross died under the old covenant as did anybody else that died within those three days. We can believe Jesus was who he said he was all we want but unless we also believe that he conquered death by rising from the grave on the 3rd day then one is not truly saved. That is a vital part to our salvation!

Jesus did not have to deny God or himself as he **was** God (John 10:30). The reasons I gave previously were all reasons why men go to Hell. Numbers one and three cover number two now that he is raised but since that had not happened yet, Jesus was still bound by number two. Yes, he had already died but he had not yet risen. He died just as any other man under the old covenant. It was once he had risen that the new covenant began and he was brought up into Heaven.

Now that we have a Biblical understanding of what the requirements of entry into Heaven are, we can now focus on the Biblical support for Jesus in Hell.

Ephesians 4:9-10

> (Now this expression, "He ascended," what does it mean except that He also had descended into the lower parts of the earth? He who descended is Himself also He who ascended far above all the heavens, so that He might fill all things.)

Matthew 12:40

> for just as JONAH WAS THREE DAYS AND THREE NIGHTS IN THE BELLY OF THE SEA MONSTER, so will the Son of Man be three days and three nights in the heart of the earth.

Luke 16:22-24

> "Now it came about that the poor man died and he was carried away by the angels to Abraham's Bosom; and the rich man also died and was buried. And in Hades he lifted up his eyes, being in torment, and saw Abraham far away, and Lazarus in his bosom. And he cried out and said, 'Father Abraham, have mercy on me, and send Lazarus, that he may dip the tip of his finger in water and cool off my tongue; for I am in agony in this flame.'"

During the times of Jesus, it was a normal belief that Hades was located deep within the Earth. Hades was broken into two parts. There was a place of torment and a place where there was peace. Before the death and resurrection of Christ, the faithful went to a temporary holding place of peace. The unfaithful went to a place where there was torment and suffering. This temporary holding place was not purgatory. It was not meant to work off the sins of the flesh. We also know Heaven is a place of eternity and not merely temporary. This place was meant to act as a holding area for those Old Testament saints awaiting the death and resurrection of Christ so that they might gain access to Heaven. This place was known as Paradise, or Abraham's Bosom. Those with faith were in Paradise and those without faith were in a place of tormenting flames; a precursor to the Lake of Fire called Gehenna.

To further elaborate, picture the afterlife as four separate chambers. These chambers consisted of:

1) Heaven
2) Hades (non-tormenting side)
3) Hades (tormenting side)
4) Gehenna (the actual fiery Hell)

Prior to the cross, both Heaven and Gehenna were devoid of humans. No man had been granted entrance into Heaven yet the final condemnation to the flames of Gehenna had not been carried out. Upon the resurrection of Christ, both Gehenna and the non-tormenting side of Hades were empty. While Christ redeemed those in Abraham's Bosom, those in the tormenting side of Hades remained. Their final condemnation to Gehenna still awaits. Only upon the second coming of Christ will both sides of Hades finally be empty and everyone in their eternal residence. Those with faith in Christ will continue to be in the presence of the Lord. However, those who rejected the Savior will finally see weeping and gnashing of teeth (Matthew 22:13) in the fires of Gehenna for all eternity.

Looking back at Matthew 12:40, some have tried to say it was probably speaking of a cave or a tomb in which Jesus' body was kept. This is not even remotely close to being accurate. The tomb of Jesus would have been more of a cave. The heart of the Earth is hardly a hole in a mountain. The word used for" heart" is the Greek word kardi/a| (*kardia*). It was used in the sense of being the center of the Earth and to say the entire Earth comes from it. *Kardia* is certainly not being used to speak of a tomb. It speaks of the center of the Earth. The *kardia* of the Earth is referencing Hades.

We all remember the story of the thief on the cross. Jesus said to him, "Truly I say to you, today you shall be with Me in Paradise." The thief went with Jesus, as well as all the rest of the Old Testament saints, to Hell. Yes, they went to Hell. No, they did not go to be tormented. As Jesus told us, they went to Paradise; the non-torturous part of Hades, the abode of the dead.

What do we know as of now?

5) Jesus was in the grave for 3 days.
6) Jesus descended into the lower parts of the Earth.
7) Jesus was going to be in Paradise the day of his death.
8) Jesus was in the heart of the Earth for three days and three nights.

Based on this information, we can see Jesus spent three days and three nights in the heart of the Earth. Since this was the exact same amount of time his body was in the grave, we can conclude that if he were in Paradise on one of those days, Paradise would have to be in the heart of the Earth. The only way to Heaven is through the Son. It is not simply a belief in the Son that grants us access. It is belief in who the Son is as well as belief in what took place in the death and resurrection. Before this process was complete, man had no way into Heaven. It was not until the resurrection that Paradise was relocated into Heaven and all the saints from that day forth could share in the Glory of God in Heaven.

1 Peter 3:19-20a

> In which also He went and made proclamation to the spirits now in prison, who once were disobedient,

What exactly did Jesus do during his three days in Hell? 1 Peter makes mention of Jesus proclaiming the Truth to the spirits in prison. These spirits were characterized as being disobedient. The Old Testament saints that went to Abraham's Bosom certainly were not characterized by disobedience. Their obedience & faithfulness was the thing that saved them. They just had to wait for Christ before they could enter the Kingdom of Heaven. Verse 19 also says the spirits were in prison. Prison is a place where you go as a result of wrongdoing. You break the law and you go to prison. The demons and disobedient people of the world both broke the law of God. As a result, they would have been imprisoned in Hell awaiting the final judgment of God when all of Hell is cast into the lake of fire; Gehenna (Mark 9:43, Revelation 20:14).

2 Peter 2:4

> For if God did not spare the angels when they sinned, but cast them into Hell and committed them to pits of darkness, reserved for judgment;

The fallen angels are in prison. The NASB uses the word "pits" but, if you look, the KJV uses the word "chains" in their translation. The Greek word for this was σειρά (*seira*). It literally meant a line, rope, or chain. The fallen angels, as well as disobedient people, are in chains in prison. While some translations use the word "saints" instead of "spirits" in 1 Peter 3:19, this is why I do not believe Jesus preached to the saints at all. I believe this is yet another area of mistranslation that only leads to poor doctrine and theology. I feel the NASB is spot on when it uses the word *spirits*.

Revelation 1:17-18

> When I saw Him, I fell at His feet like a dead man And He placed His right hand on me, saying, "Do not be afraid; I am the first and the

> last, and the living One; and I was dead, and behold, I am alive forevermore, and I have the keys of death and of Hades.

Jesus conquered death. Death no longer has any hold over a Christian. Sure, we will all die. The difference is that we will live in Heaven because we have been reconciled to God through Christ. Christ is the only way to Heaven. What of the people from the Old Testament? Did they go to Heaven? I would have to say no. They performed sacrifices but this was a continued action. Christ cannot be compared to an animal. He is called the Lamb of God but he was so much more than that. No mere animal could cleanse the way Christ did. I fully believe the Old Testament saints went to Paradise as a place of storage awaiting the death of Christ. Even more, I believe they stayed there until the resurrection. It was not until Jesus rose from the grave that he truly defeated death.

John 20:17, NIV

> Jesus said, "Do not hold on to me, for I have not yet returned to the Father. Go instead to my brothers and tell them, 'I am returning to my Father and your Father, to my God and your God.' "

This has commonly been misinterpreted to mean Jesus had to remain pure and did not want anyone to touch him. The problem with that interpretation is that it is in direct contradiction with John 20:27 when Jesus told Thomas to touch his wounds. In truth, Jesus was telling Mary not to cling to him. He was telling her to not expect his presence to continue for much longer for he had not yet returned to the Father but would soon be doing so. This brings me to my point. Jesus rose on the third day. Up until this point, he had not yet returned to his Father. He had not rejoined God in Heaven as of yet. Well, where was he then? He was in Paradise during this time. After the third day, he rose from the dead, saw his apostles along with hundreds of others, and joined God in Heaven.

Looking back, we see a few things:

1) the *kardia* of the Earth is Hades and not a hole in a mountain.

2) Jesus preached to the spirits in prison.

3) the spirits in prison are the fallen angels and those who rejected God.

4) Jesus had not yet returned to the Father (John 20:17).

The very basis of the disbelief in Jesus going to Hell for 3 days is:

1) People do not want to believe Paradise was a section of Hades.

2) People refuse to believe Jesus (being God) could go to Hades.

There is no Biblical evidence stating that Jesus did not go to Hell. On the other hand, the Biblical evidence is stacked saying he did. Ask yourself these questions: If he had not yet returned to the Father, where was he those 3 days? What spirits in prison was he preaching to? Why would they speak of the center of the Earth?

If he was in a tomb that whole time, he would not have been able to preach to anyone. This is another sign that the *kardia* of the Earth is not speaking of the tomb of Jesus. Jesus was preaching to the spirits in prison. He was in the *kardia* of the Earth while doing it. He had not yet returned to the Father. That only leaves one place and it makes perfect sense Biblically.

The doctrine of Jesus in Hell is a very Biblical teaching and a very accurate teaching. I do not believe he went there to suffer in pain. I believe he went there as a result of the sin of the world being on him. It was the same reason any of the other Old Testament saints went there. They placed their faith in God but they still owed the penalty of sin. Jesus was spotless up until the point that he became the ultimate sacrifice and took the sin of the world upon himself as the substitutionary atonement (2 Corinthians 5:21). He then went to Paradise and rose three days later, defeating death once for all.

10 GENDER NEUTRAL?

      Much has changed over the years. The cultural view of women has gone from lower class to upper class, lower quality to higher quality, feminine to feminist, etc. It is a subject that always seems to be changing depending on the times we are in. The same can be said for men. However, there is one constant that we can depend on. We can look to God's Holy Word for the answers.

    The Bible is not silent when it comes to the roles and responsibilities of men and women. Unfortunately, many Christians choose to skip over those parts in favor of what the world teaches. As Christians, we are called to be in the world but not of it. Instead of conforming our views to the world, we are to conform them to Christ. The only way to do this is by conforming our views to that of Scripture.

    1 Corinthians has a lot to say on the subject of men and women. In fact, it has so much to say on the matter that many in the church today, corrupted by the world, refuse to acknowledge it as truth. They teach that it is sexist and was only for a particular culture. They teach that to follow the same practice today would be to take 10 steps back in the progress we have made regarding women's rights and equality. The problem is that these people have no idea what Scripture really

says. The bigger problem is that they are forsaking the truth in lieu of worldly wisdom and are threatening a design that God created. The simple truth of the matter can be found in 1 Corinthians 11:3.

1 Corinthians 11:3

> But I want you to understand that Christ is the head of every man, and the man is the head of a woman, and God is the head of Christ.

Paul apparently knew this was an issue that he had to carefully explain. We can see it in his wording of, "But I want you to understand…" We can see a sense of importance but we also see a sense of sensitivity. It was a touchy subject but it needed to be taught. As with back then, it is a touchy subject even today. Nobody wants to hear that because it sounds sexist. However, further examination shows a much different story. Instead of being sexist, it is actually an honor.

If we left it at saying man is the head of every woman, it would be incomplete. It goes on to say God is the head of Christ. If the Bible were putting down women, one would have to conclude it is putting down Christ as well. Christ was a wonderful leader but he was also the ultimate role model in submissiveness. He was submissive to the Father unto the point of death! Through his submissiveness, salvation is possible. Here, we see submissiveness being painted in an entirely different light from what the world describes.

Furthermore, it says Christ is the head of every man. God submits to nobody, man submits to Christ, and woman submits to man. All have a very important purpose in their submission. As we already covered, Christ submitted to the Father for the purpose of salvation and reconciliation. Now, we are going to get into the roles of man and woman regarding submissiveness and headship.

Christ was submissive to the Father yet men are to submit to him. This is because he holds absolute authority.

Ephesians 1:22-23

> And He put all things in subjection under His feet, and gave Him as head over all things to the church, which is His body, the fullness of Him who fills all in all.

Matthew 28:18

> And Jesus came up and spoke to them, saying, "All authority has been given to Me in heaven and on earth.

Not only does God have a plan as outlined in 11:3, we are also commanded to show a sign of our roles.

1 Corinthians 11:4-5

> Every man who has something on his head while praying or prophesying disgraces his head. But every woman who has her head uncovered while praying or prophesying disgraces her head, for she is one and the same as the woman whose head is shaved.

We see the basic concept here is that man is to remain uncovered while praying or prophesying yet women are to remain covered. At first, this can seem a little confusing. To fully understand it, we need to look at the bigger picture.

1 Corinthians 11:14-15

> Does not even nature itself teach you that if a man has long hair, it is a dishonor to him, but if a woman has long hair, it is a glory to her? For her hair is given to her for a covering.

We can clearly see women are being described as having a natural covering of their long hair whereas men are not. In the same way, this is the idea behind the symbol of a covering. Some form of head covering was to be used by women as a symbol of submission. While this is seen as ludicrous in America today, many places in the world still subscribe to this practice. When I went on a mission trip to Ukraine, this was a part of the briefing. The women out there wear a covering, often a cloth wrap, around their head. It is out of the ordinary when someone does **not** do this. The purpose of verses 4 to 5 telling men not to wear a head covering and women to have their head covered is another way of telling us not to cross over into the roles of the other gender. It is disgraceful for a man to take on the role of a woman and vice versa. The head covering is the woman's outward symbol of submission within the church under God.

While it may not seem like a big deal to us, Paul makes it known to be a very big deal.

1 Corinthians 11:5-6

> But every woman who has her head uncovered while praying or prophesying disgraces her head, for she is one and the same as the woman whose head is shaved. For if a woman does not cover her head, let her also have her hair cut off; but if it is disgraceful for a woman to have her hair cut off or her head shaved, let her cover her head.

To get the full effect, we need to understand what a woman with a shaved head meant. A woman with a shaved head was a sign of a prostitute. It was meant to be a public symbol of shame. Much the opposite, a head covering is meant to be a public symbol of honor and obedience. If a woman desires to not have her head covered in church, let her shave her head and look like a prostitute. If she does not want to look like a prostitute and be associated with prostitution, let her cover her head. It was as simple as that.

This leads us to question why only women had their head covered if both women and men are submissive to some higher authority. The answer to this one is also found in Scripture.

1 Corinthians 11:7-10

> For a man ought not to have his head covered, since he is the image and glory of God; but the woman is the glory of man. For man does not originate from woman, but woman from man; for indeed man was not created for the woman's sake, but woman for the man's sake. Therefore the woman ought to have a symbol of authority on her head, because of the angels.

Genesis 1:26

> Then God said, "Let Us make man in Our image, according to Our likeness; and let them rule over the fish of the sea and over the birds of the sky and over the cattle and over all the earth, and over every creeping thing that creeps on the earth."

Simply put, man is made in the image of God whereas woman is made in the image of man. God is the Supreme Authority. He submits to no one. Men are made in the image of God. We submit to God but we do not wear a head covering. Our gender alone symbolizes our role. Man is proof of the glory of God and what He can create. However, women are made in the image and glory of man and what can be created from man. While it sounds sexist, it is still God's plan and we know God is good in all ways.

We see in verse 10 that it says a woman should have her head covered because of the angels. This is a subject that has always had differing opinions. You look in 10 different commentaries and you will find 5 different opinions. This is because the other 5 authors chose not to even touch the subject and skipped over it instead. When looked at in the full context, it isn't that difficult to understand. In fact, it is quite simple.

Angels are created beings meant to worship, submit to, and serve God. That is their whole purpose for existence. They are used by God in any way He chooses. However, in the beginning, a third of the angels decided to follow Lucifer. Lucifer desired to be like God (Isaiah

14:14) and he convinced many angels to follow him. This was the ultimate act of disobedience and refusal to submit to authority. As a result, Lucifer and the fallen angels were cast out of Heaven by God. This should be remembered by all. It should always be in the back of our mind to show the importance of submission. Because of the incident that took place in the beginning, always submit to the authority placed over you and do it gladly.

So far this entire lesson makes God out to be a male chauvinist. This couldn't be any further from the truth.

1 Corinthians 11:11-12

> However, in the Lord, neither is woman independent of man, nor is man independent of woman. For as the woman originates from the man, so also the man has his birth through the woman; and all things originate from God.

It was important for Paul to teach on this as well. It is very easy to get carried away with the previous verses and take on a position of a master with his servants. This is **not** the design God created. While it is true that woman was made from man and is the glory of man, without woman, man would cease to exist. She has a very important role that God has blessed her with. Equality was important even back then.

John MacArthur has a great way of explaining the importance of headship and submission among men and women in the church.

John MacArthur

> [Paul] makes no distinction between men and women as far as personal worth, abilities, intellect, or spirituality are concerned. Both as human beings and as Christians, women in general are completely equal to men spiritually. Some women obviously are even superior to some men in abilities, intellect, maturity, and spirituality. God established the principle of male authority and female subordination for the purpose of order and complementation, not on the basis of and innate superiority of males. An employee may be more intelligent and more skilled than his boss, but a company cannot be run without submission to proper authority,

> even if some of those in authority are not as capable as they ought to be. [i]

Just because man is placed over woman in headship does not mean man is better. It just means that is the way God designed it and we are to follow it because it is His will. Unfortunately, many men and women fall short in this because of the world's influence. Satan has crept into the Church in many ways and this is yet another one of them. If he can't take something out of Scripture, he will try his hardest to get people to misinterpret it so that they will think it no longer applies and was strictly cultural. This is the belief of many female pastors today.

1 Corinthians 14:34

> The women are to keep silent in the churches; for they are not permitted to speak, but are to subject themselves, just as the Law also says.

Many have taken this to mean that women are not allowed to speak in church at all. Because of this, they either look down at women or take the passage to be invalid today. We must never take a single verse and attempt to interpret it on our own. We must always take Scripture as a whole. Let's look at the entire passage in context.

1 Corinthians 14:31-35

> For you can all prophesy one by one, so that all may learn and all may be exhorted; and the spirits of prophets are subject to prophets; for God is not a God of confusion but of peace, as in all the churches of the saints. The women are to keep silent in the churches; for they are not permitted to speak, but are to subject themselves, just as the Law also says. If they desire to learn anything, let them ask their own husbands at home; for it is improper for a woman to speak in church.

We can see it is not saying women are to remain silent in all forms. We can clearly see it is referring to prophecy. However, if you will remember, 1 Corinthians 11:5 tells a woman to have her head covered if she is going to prophesy. Why the apparent contradiction? It is because people fail to properly interpret what is being said.

First of all, if you read chapter 7 of this book, you will recall that prophecy was not just telling the future but was actually a gift of proclaiming publicly the truth of God and was not limited to new revelation but was often the already existing Word. Women are not prohibited from speaking out and teaching the Word. If you look again, 11:5 does not mention the church. It is speaking in general. There is nothing to prohibit a woman from teaching. In fact, women are all over the Old and New Testament with teaching examples. Women are free to teach all women studies. They are free to teach children. They are free to minister alongside their husbands as Aquila and Priscilla did in Scripture. However, in accordance with 1 Corinthians 14, a woman is never to be in that position of authority when placed over men in a church environment. She is to subject herself to man. If she desires to speak forth in a church environment for the purpose of edifying the church and teaching the church, let her do it at home with her husband. This is not to say men cannot learn anything from women. To claim this would be arrogant and bull-headed. Many women, especially in today's society, have seminary degrees. A man should not think so highly of himself to the point where he refuses to learn from someone solely based on their gender. However, the level of knowledge does not determine the structure of authority. The concept of female pastors, which is becoming more and more accepted, is a highly unbiblical concept.

Even the people of Corinth apparently thought it was a cultural thing Paul was teaching as he felt the need to squash this idea.

1 Corinthians 11:16

> But if one is inclined to be contentious, we have no other practice, nor have the churches of God.

It was not just something that belonged to another region. It was not something that belonged to another time period. Paul says if anyone is inclined to be contentious, if anyone desires to argue his teaching as cultural, there is no other practice in all the churches of God. Every single church of God practices these things. Obviously, the church in Corinth was a valid church of God. What Paul is saying is that anybody who claims to follow God should incorporate these practices into their local body as well. It was not a standard of man in a local church. It was a standard of God that He set forth for the Church as a whole to follow. We may not like it because of our culture but it is still the Word of God regardless and as stated in the beginning, it is not a sign of dishonor but rather, a symbol of honor.

This honor carries over into marriage as well.

Ephesians 5:22-24

> Wives, be subject to your own husbands, as to the Lord. For the husband is the head of the wife, as Christ also is the head of the church, He Himself being the Savior of the body. But as the church is subject to Christ, so also the wives ought to be to their husbands in everything.

This is another area that is horribly misinterpreted as well as avoided in today's culture. Wives look at it and say nobody can tell them what to do or control them. Men look at it and think they have absolute control over their wives in all things. Both of these are erroneous. In fact, Paul clarifies this with a very strong stipulation.

Ephesians 5:25-30

> Husbands, love your wives, just as Christ also loved the church and gave Himself up for her, so that He might sanctify her, having cleansed her by the washing of water with the word, that He might present to Himself the church in all her glory, having no spot or wrinkle or any such thing; but that she would be holy and blameless. So husbands ought also to love their own wives as their own bodies.

> He who loves his own wife loves himself; for no one ever hated his own flesh, but nourishes and cherishes it, just as Christ also does the church, because we are members of His body.

Husbands are to love their wives just a Christ loved the Church. Christ loved the Church to the point of death. In a recent lesson, we covered the different types of love in the Greek language. The type of love portrayed here is agape love. It was totally selfless and sacrificial. This is the same type of love we are to have for our wives. We are given authority over our wives so that we may flourish; not have a servant. We are to love our wives just as we love ourselves. In fact, we are to love our wives greater than we love ourselves just as Christ loved the Church greater than himself.

Ephesians 5:33

> Nevertheless, each individual among you also is to love his own wife even as himself, and the wife must see to it that she respects her husband.

In many polls over the years, a simple question has been posed: "Would you rather feel loved or respected?" The majority of men say they would rather feel respected while the majority of women say they would rather feel loved. Typically, a man feels loved when he has genuine respect while a woman feels respected when she feels genuinely loved but it does not work the other way around for either party. These results are not surprising. In fact, they were not surprising even during the time that Paul was writing to the church of Ephesus. This is why it does not tell men to respect their wives and for wives to love their husbands. Women are to respect their husbands through submission in all areas. Husbands are to love their wives sacrificially and ensure she feels it and is taken care of. Through the love shown by the husband, the wife will have a desire to submit because she will know she is taken care of and that the authority is not being abused. The results of the poll are based on our emotional responses and needs. These are controlled by nature itself. It is only when our culture gets in the way that we reject nature to look for an alternative way. Unfortunately, these alternative ways will fail.

Galatians 3:27-28

> For all of you who were baptized into Christ have clothed yourselves with Christ. There is neither Jew nor Greek, there is neither slave nor free man, there is neither male nor female; for you are all one in Christ Jesus.

Again, in God's eyes, man and woman are equal. There is nothing in His plan that makes one superior to the other. They are not independent of each other. There is simply a design of authority and submission that must be followed in the Church if we claim to be followers of His Word. Stop trying to find another way and look at Scripture for what it is in the proper light. God created an order and He saw that it was good. Who are we to say otherwise?

---

[i] John MacArthur, The MacArthur New Testament Commentary on First Corinthians [Moody Publishers, 1984] pg. 254

11 LOVE SOMEONE INTO HELL

Right about now you are probably asking yourself if this is even possible. I'm sure we have all seen the "Turn or burn" type of evangelists out there just as we have all seen the "lifestyle evangelism" types. Each side typically feels the other is wrong. The fire and brimstone evangelists feel they need to warn others and that to take a soft approach just isn't effective enough. Just the same, the softer side evangelists feel the need to express love without scaring potential converts away. Both types have fallen prey to modern television. One side is cast as a paranoid group with no capacity for love. The other side is shown as a weak and timid group that often gets bullied or laughed at.

Many say it is unloving to be harsh when speaking the Truth. They say Christians need to be more loving and gentle and what we are doing is unbiblical because Jesus wants us to show love. Others say if we are too gentle, it waters down the Truth. They say that such a method is unbiblical and feel the need to proclaim the Truth with power and authority. While we know that neither side feels the other is right in their methodology, the purpose of this chapter is to find out what the Bible has to say on the matter. Does Scripture teach us to be stern in our approach and leave gentleness behind or vice versa?

2 Timothy 3:16

> All scripture is given by inspiration of God, and is profitable for doctrine, **for reproof**, for correction, for instruction in righteousness:

Let's look at the word reproof:

reproof - ἔλεγχος – elegchos

1) a proof, that by which a thing is proved or tested
2) conviction

This alone tells us that Scripture is to convict us. We are to use it to play off of the convictions of others. This is one profitable use. It does not, however, tell us whether it is to be harsh or soft tongued. To get to this, we must look at the root word.

rebuke - ἐλέγχω – elegchō

1) to convict, refute, confute
   a) generally with a suggestion of shame of the person convicted
2) by conviction to bring to the light, to expose
   a) by word
3) to reprehend severely, chide, admonish, reprove
4) to call to account, show one his fault, demand an explanation
   a) by deed
5) to chasten, to punish

Elegchō deals with conviction through severe chastening and lecturing. This word was not used in a gentle manner. It was very harsh in nature. This does not mean it is unloving. We are in Christ therefore we know we are to love one another. Paul rebuked his Church on numerous occasions. If someone did that today, many people would claim he was unloving and only pushing people away. This couldn't be further from the truth. Imagine a Bible filled with stories of people using nothing but lifestyle evangelism. How about a rendering of Paul being gentle in his approach to the Corinthians? This just didn't happen. He convicted them and rebuked them harshly but it was in deep love.

The word *elegchos* comes from this root meaning. 2 Timothy 3:16 gives us the green light to speak harshly if need be but the rest of Scripture ties in by telling us in needs to be done in love. Does this mean the people being gentle are wrong? Of course not! Jesus was gentle in so many of his messages. He was also harsh when he made a ruckus in the temple. Neither is wrong. They are both very useful.

You can gently instruct somebody by severe conviction through bold truth. With a fellow Christian, we can tell them they are wrong and even humiliate them if, sadly, the level of church discipline gets to this point. This is a Biblical method. Matthew 18:17 tells us to treat such a person as a "Gentile or tax collector." Both were despised and viewed as lower class beings in the sight of the Jews. While Christ is not condoning bigotry, he is condoning a method of extreme humiliation as a tool to bring this person back into fellowship upon repentance. For a non-Christian, they do not know any better. We are still to speak boldly with authority. That part is not to be watered down. However, just as God has much longsuffering towards us, we are to have the same patience toward non-Christians. Does this mean we are to water anything down with the purpose of tickling the ears? Certainly not! We are still to boldly proclaim the Truth!

Ephesians 2:19-20

> And the Lord's bond-servant must not be quarrelsome, but be kind to all, able to teach, patient when wronged, with gentleness correcting those who are in opposition, if perhaps God may grant them repentance leading to the knowledge of the truth, and they may come to their senses and escape from the snare of the devil,

> having been held captive by him to do his will.

    Understand that it is entirely possible to be harsh on someone up to the point where they stop listening. A good teacher must use discernment and wisdom to understand when a situation calls for a stern approach and when it calls for a softer approach. Just keep in mind that we can also be too gentle and love someone straight into Hell because we never spoke the Truth with power and authority as 2 Timothy 3:16 grants us permission to do.

12 GOOD WORKS

Imagine you are on the street witnessing to the strangers around you. You ask each person whether not they feel they will go to Heaven when they die. How many of those people do you think will say yes? Furthermore, how many of those people will justify their answer by saying they feel they are a "good person?"

Unfortunately, being a good person is not what brings us salvation. This is one of the most believed lies in the world today. Saving faith in Christ is the only way to be reconciled to God.

John 3:20

> "For everyone who does evil hates the light, and does not come to the light, lest is deeds should be exposed.

Matthew 19:17

> And He said to him, "Why are you asking Me about what is good? There is only One who is good; but if you wish to enter into life, keep the commandments."

Without Christ, we are separated from God. Only God is good. This is not saying it is impossible to do good at all. It is saying without God, it is impossible to do good. As a result, the man who is lacking in God, who hides from the Light, is incapable of performing an action which is truly good when judged by the righteous standard of God.

The Greek word used for "good" in Matthew 19:17 is *agathos* (ἀγαθός). It speaks of a good nature, honorable, distinguished, upright, and excellent. Not one is like this except God (Ecclesiastes 17:20). We all have our sinful nature to us. This does not mean we are incapable of doing good. Of ourselves, no good can exist but when God is the focus, good will flourish.

1 Thessalonians 4:7

> For God has not called us for the purpose of impurity, but in sanctification.

Before Christ came into our life, we were not capable of doing good. We were lost. This is the exact state of much of the world today. Many claim to be believers yet do not understand what faith is about. They know OF God but do not KNOW God. It is because of this fact that they are incapable of doing good.

An unbeliever is capable of looking good in the eyes of the world but God does not share the same standards. While one man may see a hero, God may see a worker of iniquity (Luke 13:27).

Isaiah 64:6a

> "For all of us have become like one who is unclean,

> And all our righteous deeds are like a filthy garment;

Isaiah drives home the point of how filthy our righteous deeds really are. In the original Hebrew, he uses the word `**ed** (du@). The literal translation used here means "and like rags used of menstruation." Even our greatest works, when Christ is not the center, are like the rags used to catch the blood of a menstruating woman. Works alone are worthless. They are not good. Nothing is good unless it is of God. A non-Christian can do all the "good" things they want but they will be in vain. They can donate to as many charities, visit as many retirement homes, or do as much volunteer work as they want but the works will never be good in nature. On the bright side, when Christ is our focus, all our works become righteous because they are based in his love.

When we are saved, we are changed forever. We have a new calling from this point on. We are no longer called to be lost in this world. We are called to be sanctified. We are called to be holy. We are called to be set aside for God.

Ephesians 2:10

> For we are His workmanship, created in Christ Jesus for good works, which God prepared beforehand so that we would walk in them.

We are created as new creatures for the very purpose of doing good for God. We take our holy and sanctified selves and finally do good for the first time in our lives.

A Christian and a non-Christian can take the same exact works. They can both go to retirement homes. They can both give to charities. They can both volunteer their time to causes. Only one of these will truly be doing good. The other will be performing works no better than filthy rags. It is not the Christian that makes these works good. It is the fact that they are being performed for God. They are being performed with God in mind and with God's purpose in mind. This alone makes the works good.

Go back to the scenario I had you imagine at the beginning of this chapter. Remember all the people who believed in God? Remember all the people who thought they would go to Heaven and be with God because they were good people? Scripture addresses these people.

Luke 13:25-28

> "Once the head of the house gets up and shuts the door, and you begin to stand outside and knock on the door, saying, 'Lord, open up to us!' then He will answer and say to you, 'I do not know where you are from.' "Then you will begin to say, 'We ate and drank in Your presence, and You taught in our streets'; and He will say, 'I tell you, I do not know where you are from; DEPART FROM ME, ALL YOU EVILDOERS.' "In that place there will be weeping and gnashing of teeth when you see Abraham and Isaac and Jacob and all the prophets in the kingdom of God, but yourselves being thrown out.

This is a prime example of people who thought they were doing good. They did many things in the "name of God" but none of it was **for** God or **through** God. In verse 27, the NASB uses the word evildoers. This is a very apt description because without God, nothing is good. There are many things that we would classify as good on this earth but from the perspective of God, one's nature cannot produce these good works. Only evil results; filthy rags are the result. The only way true good can be done is if it comes from God or through God from us. The only way we can do good is if we are created as new creatures in Christ. The KJV does not use the word evildoers. It uses the word iniquity.

<u>iniquity</u> - *adikia* - ἀδικία

1) injustice, of a judge
2) unrighteousness of heart and life
3) a deed violating law and justice, act of unrighteousness

Adikia comes from the root word *adikos*.

<u>adikos</u> - ἄδικος

1) descriptive of one who violates or has violated justice
   a) unjust
   b) unrighteous, sinful
   c) of one who deals fraudulently with others, deceitful

Both words are fitting. Though the KJV makes it sound more eloquent, the NASB pretty much sums it all into 1 word...EVILDOER.

As much as one thinks they are doing good in this world, they have to realize that it is **only** in this world where it will be recognized. Jesus says himself that all who claim to do good (without being a new creature in Christ) are evildoers.

13 WHERE DOES FAITH COME FROM?

This may sound like a rather obvious question but you would be surprised how many people get it all wrong. The dictionary defines faith as belief that is not based on proof. Where does this faith come from? Is it a product of a decision we make or is it something more?

Ephesians 2:8-9

> For by grace you have been saved through **faith**; and that not of yourselves, it is the **gift of God**; <u>not as a result of works</u>, so that no one may boast.

How do we normally get gifts? We either ask for them or they are given without any influence from us. The latter half of the verse tells us it was given to us without any influence on our part. There was no work done by us (praying, asking, doing good, etc). It was given as a gift out of God's own heart. He chose to give the gift of faith without any work on our part whatsoever.

You have seen the dictionary's definition of faith. What is the Biblical definition?

Hebrews 11:1, NIV

> Now faith is being sure of what we hope for and certain of what we do not see.

Some look at this verse and focus on the "we" without focusing on the rest of Scripture. The problem is that there are also many verses that say how impossible it is for one to seek God out of their own hearts. That combined with Ephesians 2:8-9 should be enough to prove faith is not something we earn or reach out for. It is something God gives us of His own Will. Faith may be something we have but it certainly is not something we create. Faith is not a result of anything on our part.

I say there are plenty of verses regarding the origin. I would like to take this time to make mention of a few of those verses. All emphasis is mine.

John 3:5-7

> Jesus answered, "Truly, truly, I say to you, unless one is born of the water and the Spirit he cannot enter into the kingdom of God. **That which is born of the flesh is flesh, and that which is born of the Spirit is spirit.** Do not be amazed that I said to you, 'You must be born again.'"

Romans 8:7-8

> because the mind set on the flesh is hostile toward God; for it does not subject itself to the law of God, for it is not even able to do so, and those who are in the flesh cannot please God.

1 Corinthians 2:14

> But a **natural man does not accept the things of the Spirit of God**, for they are foolishness to him; and he cannot **understand them**, because they are spiritually appraised.

Luke 11:23a

> He who is not with Me is against Me

We are all born into flesh. As natural man, not only is it impossible to understand the things of God (spiritually appraised), but it is also impossible to please God. It is impossible to submit to God. We are naturally hostile towards God. We are not for God, therefore we are against God. How then can one believe we make the choice to follow God of our own free will when it is impossible to understand and we are in a state of hostility?

John 8:44a

> You are of your father the devil, and you want to do the desires of your father.

2 Timothy 2:24-26

> The Lord's bond-servant must not be quarrelsome, but be kind to all, able to teach, patient when wronged, with gentleness correcting those who are in opposition, if **perhaps God may grant them repentance leading to the knowledge of the truth, and they may come to their senses** and escape from the snare of the devil, having been held captive by him to do his will.

As natural man, we desire to do the devil's work. This passage is not speaking of rebuking fellow believers. It is referring to **correcting** non-believers. It says we are to witness to non-Christians in case God decides to grant them repentance. Notice they do not come to their senses before God grants them repentance. The gift is given first. Only then will their desires change, not first. God makes the first move.

Job 14:4

Who can make the clean out of the unclean? **No one!**

Jeremiah 13:23

Can the Ethiopian change his skin

Or the leopard his spots?

Then you also can do good

Who are accustomed to doing evil.

Matthew 7:16-18

"You will know them by their fruits. Grapes are not gathered from thorn bushes nor figs from thistles, are they? So every good tree bears good fruit, but the **bad tree bears bad fruit.** A good tree cannot produce bad fruit, **nor can a bad tree produce good fruit.**"

John 6:44a

No one can come to Me unless the **Father who sent me draws him**

John 6:65

> And He was saying, "For this reason I have said to you, that no one can come to Me unless it has been **granted him from the Father.**"

2 Corinthians 3:5

> Not that we are adequate in ourselves to consider anything as coming from ourselves, but our **adequacy is from God**,

Ezekiel 36:26-27

> "Moreover, **I will give you a new heart and put a new spirit within you**; and I will remove the heart of stone from your flesh and give you a heart of flesh. **I will put My Spirit within you and cause you to walk in My statutes**, and you will be careful to observe My ordinances.

Before we move on, let's review what was just said:

1) We cannot clean ourselves any more than a leopard can change his spots.
2) One who does evil cannot also do good.
3) A bad tree will only produce bad fruit. There will be no good fruit produced by one who is unsaved.
4) The Father draws and grants. Without these, nobody can enter the kingdom of God.
5) Our adequacy is from God alone and not from our own choices.
6) God gives us a new heart. He gives us the Holy Spirit to walk in His ways. Before this, we were nothing but bad fruit incapable of doing good.

We cannot change our desires. We cannot change our hostility towards God. We are the way we are and we cannot change ourselves. Only God can make the change. Only God can *initiate* the change. Furthermore, the desire to change ourselves will not be present apart from the Spirit of God in His regenerating work.

Sinclair B. Ferguson

> We cannot think clearly about or desire Christ by our own unaided decision. Why not? We cannot respond to the good news of the gospel until we want Christ, and we cannot want Christ simply by a decision we can take at any moment we choose. We cannot say to our will, "Will, will to belong to the Lord!" It is beyond our powers to do that. No one can will the will to will what it will not will![1]

2 Corinthians 5:17-18

> Therefore if anyone is in Christ, he is a new creature; the old things are passed away; behold, new things have come. **Now all these things are from God**, who reconciled us to Himself through Christ and **gave us the ministry of reconciliation**,

Everything is from God. He draws us to Himself. He changes us. He grants repentance and an understanding of Truth. He removes hostility. He causes us to die to flesh and to be born to Spirit. He is Almighty God and it is all in His hands.

Faith may be a gift from God (Eph 2:8-9) but that is an incomplete statement regarding non-Christians. It is not just faith that God gives us but faith **in Him**. The Bible tells us that nobody seeks God (Psalm 14:2-3) and that without His gift of faith, it is impossible to understand the things of God. People can still have faith but that faith will always be misplaced unless God allows them to open their eyes and have faith in Him.

I certainly do believe it is possible to have more faith than another person even if that faith is misplaced. The great news is that faith the size of a mustard seed can move mountains if it is placed in God. Faith placed in anything else will be empty regardless how big it is.

Be encouraged! Have faith!

---

[i] Sinclair B. Ferguson, By Grace Alone: How the Grace of God Amazes Me [Reformation Trust Publishing, 2010] pg. 4

14 THREE SIMPLE WORDS

I want to start out by asking a question. I'm just going to mention three simple words and I want you to put them in chronological order. While contemplating the order in which you believe these words should be placed, I ask you to truly question what the words actually mean. The words are:

1) Grace

2) Faith

3) Regeneration

If you had to place a chronological order on those three words, what order would you put them in? In my personal experience, most people place them in the order of grace, faith, and then regeneration. The reasoning is that God must first give us grace but then we choose whether to accept His gift before any regeneration can occur. I hope by the end of this chapter, you will be able to see that this is a false doctrine that has infiltrated the Church and confused many well-intentioned believers; many of whom are not even aware they are confused. While it is not my recommendation that you reject your fellow brother or sister in Christ over this, one should still be aware of the depth of this doctrine and how it lays the foundation for one's entire understanding of who God is and what He has done for you. It is my hope that by the end of this chapter, you will be able to fully (or at least begin to) understand the proper order of these three words.

Acts 15:11

> But we believe that we are saved through the **grace** of the Lord Jesus, in the same way as they also are.

Acts 18:27

> And when he wanted to go across to Achaia, the brethren encouraged him and wrote to the disciples to welcome him; and when he had arrived, he greatly helped those who had believed through **grace**.

Romans 3:24

> being justified as a gift by His **grace** through the redemption which is in Christ Jesus;

Ephesians 2:8

> For by **grace** you have been saved through faith; and that not of yourselves, it is the gift of God;

Grace is completely God's doing. It is His gift to us, as Christians and it is the backbone of our salvation. We are saved through grace, believe through grace, and are justified by grace. God is a gracious God (Psalm 86:15, Jonah 4:2)! Ephesians 2:8 tells us that we are saved through faith by **grace**. Grace has to take place before any faith can.

Romans 9:23

> And He did so to make known the riches of His glory upon vessels of mercy, which He prepared beforehand for glory,

God showered His grace upon us before the foundation of the world. Before anything ever was, He had a plan. Part of that plan was to call the vessels of mercy to Himself. Even while we were still enemies of God, He showed His love for us and lavished us with grace (Romans 5:8, Ephesians 1:8). The fact that grace comes first is not usually the part that confuses people. It is the proper order of faith and regeneration that gets sticky. As I have already stated, this is not the correct order at all.

Psalm 53:2-3

> God has looked down from heaven upon the sons of men
> > To see if there is anyone who understands,
> > Who seeks after God.
>
> Every one of them has turned aside; together they have become corrupt;
> > There is no one who does good, not even one.

Luke 9:23

> And He was saying to *them* all, "If anyone wishes to come after Me, he must deny himself, and take up his cross daily and follow Me.

While some claim a conditional statement implies a necessary choice, this is not always so. Oftentimes, as is the case here, it only necessitates a requirement. However, a requirement does not always necessitate an ability to fulfill it.

First of all, it is impossible for one to choose God. Before salvation, we serve the dominion of Satan (Acts 26:18). We are at war with God and hate Him (John 3:20a). Nobody chooses the enemy. Even the most infamous traitors in American history were not serving the enemy. They may have been OUR enemy, but they were not THEIR enemy. Whether it was money, allegiance, or some other common bond, our enemy had become their ally. In the same way, nobody who chooses God is an enemy of God at the time. In order for one to choose God, a change must first occur. There must be a common bond.

Ephesians 2:1

> And you were dead in your trespasses and sins,

Ephesians 2:5

> even when we were dead in our transgressions, made us alive together with Christ (by grace you have been saved),

Colossians 2:13

> When you were dead in your transgressions and the uncircumcision of your flesh, He made you alive together with Him, having forgiven us all our transgressions,

Paul not only tells us we are at war with God, hate God, and belong to Satan. He takes it a step further and tells us we are dead in our sins. Opponents of pre-faith regeneration are forced to take verses such as these and manipulate them to say what they want. Even some of the staunchest literalists have changed these passages to say we are almost dead or are currently in a state of dying. This might sound nice except for one simple fact. It says we are already dead! The dead man does not choose to come back to life. Even Lazarus had no control over when he would be raised from the dead. In fact, Jesus left him there to rot for four days before raising him! Those who are spiritually dead can control when they are raised any more than Lazarus.

1 Corinthians 2:14

> But a natural man does not accept the things of the Spirit of God, for they are foolishness to him; and he cannot understand them, because they are spiritually appraised.

We see this verse speaking of the natural man. The natural man is a man of his own desires. He is a man at war with God. He is the unregenerate man bound by the chains of sin who still serves the dominion of Satan. Scripture tells us plainly that this man cannot understand the things of the Spirit.

2 Corinthians 5:17

> Therefore if anyone is in Christ, he is a new creature; the old things passed away; behold, new things have come.

Titus 3:5

> He saved us, not on the basis of deeds which we have done in righteousness, but according to His mercy, by the washing of regeneration and renewing by the Holy Spirit,

Here we see a new kind of person being introduced. This is the regenerate man. This man has been set free of the chains of sin. He has turned his eyes to the Light (Acts 26:18). He has been renewed by the Holy Spirit.

1 Corinthians 6:19

> Or do you not know that your body is a temple of the Holy Spirit who is in you, whom you have from God, and that you are not your own?

The Holy Spirit does not reside in the natural, unregenerate man. The Holy Spirit resides only in the regenerate man. Our bodies are the very dwelling place of the Holy Spirit; of God. Having the Holy Spirit is synonymous with being saved. It is utterly impossible for a man to be saved without the Holy Spirit. It is equally as impossible for a man's body to be the dwelling place of the Holy Spirit if he has not been regenerated. As a result, there is no way faith can come before regeneration.

First, the grace of God is poured out to us. This occurred before the foundation of the world. Next, in God's timing, we are washed anew and regenerated by the Holy Spirit. At this time, we become a new creature in Christ. We now possess the ability to understand the things of the Spirit because the Spirit resides within us. Lastly, faith occurs. It is only after grace and regeneration that one can truly have faith in God. Of course, this means the "choice" we made was not really our own but rather an irresistible calling of God Almighty as He had already changed our very nature and desires. I am thankful for this because if it were up to me and my own works (a choice is technically a work as it is something we are doing), I would be left with nothing but filthy rags (Isaiah 64:6) and a lack of Christ.

15 ONE WAY STREET

The world is a confused place. It seems everybody has their own idea of who God really is. Some believe He is nature. Some believe He is a statue. Some believe He is non-existent. Some believe He is universal. Everybody has their belief however, not all beliefs of God are based on God's own Word. Scripture tells us much of who God is. It also tells us much of how we are reconciled to Him. In fact, it goes into specifics that are so detailed, it is a wonder that anybody who claims to believer in the Bible could ever miss it.

Universalism has become very popular in our society. Nobody wants to believe in a God who would send people to Hell simply because they have a different belief from Christians. Wouldn't that be unfair? Wouldn't it be wrong for God to send everybody from a secluded tribe to Hell when they never had a chance to hear the Gospel? Isn't it kind of arrogant to say ones belief is superior to another?

I'd like to go back to one of the questions I just asked. While they were rhetorical in my usage of them, they are very real questions that have been posed to me by others. The question is, "Wouldn't it be wrong for God to send everyone from a secluded tribe to Hell when they never had a chance to hear the Gospel?" As is always my intent, I will reply with Scripture.

Romans 1:20

> For since the creation of the world His **invisible attributes**, His eternal power and divine nature, have been clearly seen, being **understood through <u>what has been made</u>, so that they are without excuse**.

It doesn't get any clearer. All men are without excuse. Man is held accountable to God just by the proof of nature. No man is innocent. Ignorance is no excuse.

Universalism claims that everyone will go to Heaven and that all paths lead there so long as one is sincere in their dedication to their god. It teaches that since God is all loving and is fair that He wouldn't possibly send men to Hell just because they believed something different because of the culture they grew up in. That can't possibly be their fault. God would never hold them accountable.

Muhammad Ali

> Rivers, ponds, lakes and streams – they all have different names, but they all contain water. Just as all religions do – they all contain truths.

This is dangerous thinking that leads many to Hell.

Matthew 19:24

> "Again I say to you, it is easier for a camel to go through the eye of a needle, than for a rich man to enter the kingdom of God."

Matthew 7:13-14

> Enter through the narrow gate; for the **gate is wide and the way is broad that leads to destruction, and there are many who enter** through it. For the **gate is small and the way is narrow that leads to life, and there are few** who find it.

If all roads lead to salvation, why is it that Scripture is so adamant that few will find it? Why does it say how difficult it is for one to find it? In fact, Matthew tells us that all paths lead to destruction with only one path leading to life. The Bible is very clear on this matter. With this established, the next step is to identify that life saving path.

Exodus 3:14

> God said to Moses, "**I AM** WHO I AM";

John 8:54

> Jesus said to them, "Truly, truly, I say to you, before Abraham was born, **I am**."

John 8:24

> "Therefore I said to you that you will die in your sins; for **unless you believe that I am He, you will die in your sins**."

I Am is the name God gave Himself in Exodus 3:14. While John 8:24 may say "believe that I am He," the original Greek did not have the word "He." This was later added in for clarity. The literal translation would be, "unless you believe that I Am, you will die in your sins." This was Jesus himself claiming his deity. He was claiming to be God Almighty by claiming to be I Am.

John 1:1

In the beginning was the Word, and the Word was with God, and **the Word was God**.

John 8:58

Jesus said to them, "Truly, truly, I say to you, before Abraham was born, I am."

Revelation 21:6

I am the Alpha and the Omega, **the beginning** and the end

Genesis 1:26

Then **God** said, "Let **Us** make man in Our image, according to **Our** likeness;

John makes a perfect case for the deity of Jesus. First, in Revelation 21:6, we see Jesus referring to himself as "the beginning." In John 1:1, he says the Word was in the beginning. The Word is Jesus. It tells us the Word was with God in the beginning. This aligns perfectly with Genesis 1:26. The "Us" and "Our" is referring to the Father and Son. Even as early as Genesis, we see 2 of the 3 Persons of the Trinity. The Son is God. How do we know this? It's because John 1:1 tells us so.

While the deity of Christ usually comes into question with Universalists, this is not always the case. Sometimes, they simply believe that Jesus is only one of the many ways to Heaven. They believe that Christians needs Jesus but a Buddhist just needs Buddha. A man recently said to me that he believes God shows Himself to mankind in different ways and that, so long as their heart is fully worshipping their God, they will still go to Heaven. While this sounds like a wonderful idea, it simply is not the truth. Truly sincere people can, and often are, sincerely wrong!

John 10:27-28

> My sheep hear My voice, and I know them, and they follow Me; and **I give** eternal life to them

Eternal life is not something that can be earned. It is not something that can be gained from some other source. It can only be obtained from Jesus if he gives it to you. But wait, can't that mean that Jesus is only one of the ways? For the answer to that, we must take Scripture as a whole.

Luke 11:23a

> He who is not with Me is against Me

John 14:6

> Jesus said to him, "I am the way, and the truth, and the life; **no one comes to the Father but through Me**.

John 12:48

> **He who rejects Me** and does not receive My sayings, **has one who**

> **judges him;**

John 5:24

> Truly, truly, I say to you, he who hears My word, and **believes Him who sent Me**, has eternal life, and **does not come into judgment**, but has passed out of death into life.

Jesus is the ONLY way to be reconciled to the Father. He is the Way, the Truth, and the Life. No man comes to the Father but through him. If one rejects Jesus, he will be judged. However, John also says if one believes in Jesus, that person will not be judged. If anybody was innocent, why would God, who knows all, feel the need to judge him as if he were charged with something? If all religions led to salvation, why would God tell us otherwise in His Holy Scripture? The only way is through Christ. Why does the man who places his faith in Christ avoid the judgment? It is because of 1 John 2:1.

1 John 2:1

> My little children, I am writing these things to you so that you may not sin And **if anyone sins, we have an Advocate** with the Father, **Jesus Christ** the righteous;

Romans 3:23 says, "For all have sinned and fall short of the glory of God." Because of this, we all deserve the judgment and wrath of God. However, Romans 5:8 says, "But God demonstrates His own love toward us, in that while we were yet sinners, Christ died for us." This brings us right back to 1 John 2:1. It is because of the death of Christ that we have an Advocate who stands between us and the judgment. It is only through Christ that one can obtain salvation. There is no other Advocate. No man can come to the Father but through the

Son for without the Son, he will perish. John 3:16 is a verse that is so often used to show the love of God but people rarely use it to show the judgment and the way of escape.

John 3:16-18

> For God so loved the world, that He gave His only begotten Son, that whoever believes in Him shall not perish, but have eternal life. For God did not send the Son into the world to judge the world, but that the world might be saved through Him. **He who believes in Him is not judged; he who does not believe has been judged already, because he has not believed in the name of the only begotten Son of God.**

1 Timothy 2:5

> For there is one God, and **one mediator** also between God and men, the man **Christ Jesus**,

Acts 4:12

> "And **there is salvation in no one else**; for there is no other name under heaven that has been given among men by which we must be saved."

1 John 2:23

> **Whoever denies the Son does not have the Father**; the one who confesses the Son has the Father also.

There is only one way to avoid the judgment and that is through Christ Jesus, the Son.

In Japan, there is a saying. They say that the road to enlightenment is like Mt Fuji; there are many ways to the top. My response is that not only are they incorrect in their theology but they aren't even on the right mountain.

Another analogy would be that of a man lost in a maze. He may truly believe all turns lead to the exit but, try as he might, he will be left with nothing but dead ends and disappointment. In reality, only one path leads to victory!

The challenge we, as Christians, face is not finding the exit. Our challenge is facing those who are still lost. It is easy to become arrogant and forget that, we too, were once lost in the maze or on the wrong mountain. Remember, it is only by the grace of God that we escaped.

1 Peter 3:15

> but sanctify Christ as Lord in your hearts, always *being* ready to make a defense to everyone who asks you to give an account for the hope that is in you, yet with gentleness and reverence;

Soli Deo Gloria!

16 A REASON TO CELEBRATE

Every Christmas season, there are a few constants. It is a time of rejoicing. It is a time for family to be together. It is a time for opening gifts. It is a time for seeing others open gifts. It is a time for setting our diets to the side. It is a time to relax. While it has become all these things, it is really so much more.

Matthew 1:18-19

> Now the birth of Jesus Christ was as follows: when His mother Mary had been betrothed to Joseph, before they came together she was found to be with child by the Holy Spirit. And Joseph her husband, being a righteous man and not wanting to disgrace her, planned to send her away secretly.

The birth of Jesus was not your average trip to the hospital. In fact, there was nothing normal in it at all. Even from the beginning, it was unique. It begins by telling us that Joseph was engaged to be married to Mary. In those days, marriages were arranged most times. The groom or his family paid a price to the bride's family. This cost covered expenses of the wedding ceremony as well as other areas. The betrothal, or *kiddushin*, was actually enough to legally bind the bride and groom in marriage. Despite this, they did not have sexual relations for quite some time to come. In some cases, this could span the course of even a year. This would not normally occur until the marriage ceremony, or *huppah*, took place. They were already in the betrothed stage but had not yet come together in a sexual sense as is indicated in the text.

Despite this, we find that Mary was found to be with child. Joseph's natural reaction was that he had been cheated on. There were a few options with him at this point.

Deuteronomy 22:23-24

> If there is a girl who is a virgin engaged to a man, and another man finds her in the city and lies with her, then you shall bring them both out to the gate of that city and you shall stone them to death; the girl, because she did not cry out in the city, and the man, because he has violated his neighbor's wife. Thus you shall purge the evil from among you.

Old Testament Law, which they were under, states Joseph had every right to take Mary out in public and stone her to death. If her adulterer was ever to be found, he would join her in death by stoning. Should he not desire her death, he could have at the very least made her ashamed for the rest of her life by leading a life marked of adultery. However, notice that Joseph does not appear to harbor any anger or resentment. He did not desire to publicly shame her or have her stoned. He was not only a righteous man. He also truly loved her. This love is evident by the fact that he desired to put her away secretly. Remember, they were already legally married although the ceremony and the consummation had not yet taken place. The word used for "send her away" literally meant a secret divorce. He loved her enough that despite being "cheated" on, he desired her safety. He would divorce her secretly and buy her some time before the public realized what had happened. However, God had other plans.

Matthew 1:20-23

> But when he had considered this, behold, an angel of the Lord appeared to him in a dream, saying, "Joseph, son of David, do not be afraid to take Mary as your wife; for the Child who has been conceived in her is of the Holy Spirit. "She will bear a Son; and you shall call His name Jesus, for He will save His people from their sins." Now all this took place to fulfill what was spoken by the Lord through the prophet: "BEHOLD, THE VIRGIN SHALL BE WITH CHILD AND SHALL BEAR A SON, AND THEY SHALL CALL HIS NAME IMMANUEL," which translated means, "GOD WITH US."

Joseph was afraid and rightly so. He assumed he had been cheated on as they had not had sexual relations yet she was pregnant. Under the Law, he was urged to have her stoned to death yet he still loved her and cared for her safety. He was about to lose his wife before the ceremony could even take place due to adultery. This, in turn, would embarrass him as well. God took all these fears and put him at ease. He sent an angel to Joseph to appear to him in a dream. This one spot in Scripture is a very important passage. He tells Joseph that Mary did not cheat on him and that the baby was actually conceived of the Holy Spirit. Joseph, being a righteous man, would have known Scripture very well. It was not simply casual reading for them. It was a way of life filled with study and memorization from childhood. The angel quoted Isaiah. The virgin birth was actually prophesied some 650 years prior. Furthermore, the name prophesied by Isaiah was Immanuel which means "God with us." This name means more than they could have guessed. Not only is God with us but he literally came to be with us in the flesh.

Matthew 1:24-25

> And Joseph awoke from his sleep and did as the angel of the Lord commanded him, and took Mary as his wife, but kept her a virgin until she gave birth to a Son; and he called His name Jesus.

Imagine the relief that must have followed upon waking! Scripture does not say he deliberated in what to do. It says he did as the angel of the Lord commanded him and he took Mary as his wife. The ceremony, or *huppah*, took place. At this point, he had every right to have sexual relations with his wife. Despite this, we are told they refrained from doing so. We are told he kept her a virgin until she gave birth to a Son. It is safe to say he did not refrain from natural marriage relations forever as the text says that it was only **until** she gave birth. Not to mention, Scripture gives the names of other children of Mary. However, Jesus was different. While Joseph was his legal father, his natural Father was of Heaven above. The baby's name was Jesus and according to the angel, he was going to save His people from their sins.

No, Jesus was not just your ordinary pregnancy and birth. He was unique in every way. It had to be so in order to fulfill the 332 specific prophecies declared all throughout the Old Testament. Jesus matched every single prophecy and not one was overlooked. This is because he is who the Bible claims him to be; God in the flesh sent not to condemn the world but to save it.

Psalm 22: 1, 7-8, 16, & 18

> My God, my God, why have You forsaken me? Far from my deliverance are the words of my groaning...... All who see me sneer at me; They separate with the lip, they wag the head, saying, "Commit yourself to the LORD; let Him deliver him; Let Him rescue him, because He delights in him."....... For dogs have surrounded me; A band of evildoers has encompassed me; They pierced my hands and my feet....... They divide my garments among them, And for my clothing they cast lots.

Matthew 27:46

> About the ninth hour Jesus cried out with a loud voice, saying, "ELI, ELI, LAMA SABACHTHANI?" that is, "MY GOD, MY GOD, WHY HAVE YOU FORSAKEN ME?"

Luke 23:35

> And the people stood by, looking on. And even the rulers were sneering at Him, saying, "He saved others; let Him save Himself if

this is the Christ of God, His Chosen One."

John 20:25 & 27

So the other disciples were saying to him, "We have seen the Lord!" But he said to them, "Unless I see in His hands the imprint of the nails, and put my finger into the place of the nails, and put my hand into His side, I will not believe."……….. Then He said to Thomas, "Reach here with your finger, and see My hands; and reach here your hand and put it into My side; and do not be unbelieving, but believing."

Matthew 27:35

And when they had crucified Him, they divided up His garments among themselves by casting lots.

Psalm 34:20

He keeps all his bones, not one of them is broken.

John 19:32

So the soldiers came, and broke the legs of the first man and of the other who was crucified with Him;

Psalm 41:9

Even my close friend in whom I trusted, who ate my bread, has lifted up his heel against me.

John 13:18

> I do not speak of all of you I know the ones I have chosen; but it is that the Scripture may be fulfilled, 'HE WHO EATS MY BREAD HAS LIFTED UP HIS HEEL AGAINST ME.'

These are only a fraction of the many prophecies of the Messiah that were fulfilled and recorded in the New Testament. All of them confirm he was who he said he was. While the timeline of his birth to his death is important, the timeline of his death to life is even more so. Let's go back to the image of Jesus on the cross.

Matthew 27:50

> And Jesus cried out again with a loud voice, and yielded up His spirit.

Mark 15:37

> And Jesus uttered a loud cry, and breathed His last.

Luke 23:46

> And Jesus, crying out with a loud voice, said, "Father, INTO YOUR HANDS I COMMIT MY SPIRIT." Having said this, He breathed His last.

John 19:30

> Therefore when Jesus had received the sour wine, He said, "It is finished!" And He bowed His head and gave up His spirit.

Have you ever really stopped to ponder the crucifixion? It was a brutal form of death. Nails were driven into your wrists and feet. You would be forced to support your body weight on either the nail in your feet or hang by the nails in your wrists. After a little while of hanging by the arms, cramps would begin to occur. The cramps would cause your chest muscles to go numb. It would be possible to breathe in but breathing out would be next to impossible. The cramps and flaming of the muscles would make it difficult to even use your legs to alleviate some of the breathing difficulties. The buildup of carbon dioxide would finally ease the cramps which would then make it possible to lift with your legs using nothing but the nail in your feet as leverage. While the pain was unbearable and it was a challenge just to breathe, this alone was not what would normally kill the person. After some time, a guard would come up and break the legs of the person hanging. This would extinguish his ability to press up with his legs so that he could breathe. While already dealing with muscles on fire and scourged flesh, he would now have to endure the pain of broken legs and the thought of knowing he would have no way to breathe. He would hang by his arms until the cramps came back. He would breathe in but not be able to breathe out. He would then die of asphyxiation.

John 19:31-33

> Then the Jews, because it was the day of preparation, so that the bodies would not remain on the cross on the Sabbath (for that Sabbath was a high day), asked Pilate that their legs might be broken, and that they might be taken away. So the soldiers came, and broke the legs of the first man and of the other who was crucified with Him; but coming to Jesus, **when they saw that He was already dead, they did not break His legs.**

While the thieves hanging on either side of Jesus both had their legs broken, Jesus was already dead. There was no need to break his legs to speed up the process. As stated above, this was a fulfillment of prophecy that no bones would be broken. However, we also see that Jesus apparently had enough energy to speak in a loud voice and speak his last important words. They were not mere whimpers or whispers.

They were loud and bold so that everybody could hear. Why then did he die so much faster than the other two? Was he weak? Not at all! If anything, it is because he was stronger than anybody could ever be. While the thieves were at the mercy of the soldiers and the cross, Jesus was at the mercy of no one but himself.

Matthew 26:51-54

> And behold, one of those who were with Jesus reached and drew out his sword, and struck the slave of the high priest and cut off his ear. Then Jesus said to him, "Put your sword back into its place; for all those who take up the sword shall perish by the sword. Or do you think that I cannot appeal to My Father, and He will at once put at My disposal more than twelve legions of angels? How then will the Scriptures be fulfilled, which say that it must happen this way?"

John 10:17-18

> "For this reason the Father loves Me, because I lay down My life so that I may take it again. **No one has taken it away from Me, but I lay it down on My own initiative** I have authority to lay it down, and I have authority to take it up again This commandment I received from My Father."

Matthew 27:50

> And Jesus cried out again with a loud voice, and **yielded up His spirit**.

It was not the cross that killed Jesus. Jesus was only on the cross because he knew what had to be done. He could have called more than twelve legions of angels to put a stop to it. To get a better idea, a legion was roughly 6,000 soldiers. In other words, Jesus said he could have instantly called more than 72,000 angels to use at his disposal. However, that was not his purpose for being on this Earth. We know from Matthew 26:38 that he was deeply grieved and had the fear of the pain he was about to go through but this did not stop him. He had a mission and there was only one way to accomplish it; death by crucifixion. Again, we see Jesus telling his disciples that nobody could take his life from him. The Father had given him the authority to lay down his own life. Matthew 27:50 aligns with this perfectly as it says Jesus yielded up his spirit. He laid down his own life and yielded up his own spirit. He did not die before the others due to being weaker. He died before the others because he chose the time at which he would yield his spirit. He fulfilled the Scripture by going to the cross, fulfilled the Scripture by speaking his final words, and yielded up his spirit at a time of his choosing to finish the fulfillment of Scripture regarding his death.

John 11:43-44

> When He had said these things, He cried out with a loud voice, "Lazarus, come forth." **The man who had died came forth**, bound hand and foot with wrappings, and his face was wrapped around with a cloth. Jesus said to them, "Unbind him, and let him go."

Acts 24:21

> other than for this one statement which I shouted out while standing among them, 'For the **resurrection of the dead** I am on trial before you today.'"

Matthew 10:5a & 8a

> These twelve Jesus sent out after instructing them:............"Heal the sick, **raise the dead**,

There were some during the apostolic age who raised the dead. They were given this authority by Christ himself. While being miraculous, the resurrection of Christ was very different.

John 10:17-18

> "For this reason the Father loves Me, because I lay down My life so that I may take it again. No one has taken it away from Me, but I lay it down on My own initiative I have authority to lay it down, and **I have authority to take it up again**. This commandment I received from My Father."

All other resurrections were performed by someone else. Christ did not need someone else. He resurrected himself. So what exactly took place during the resurrection?

1 Corinthians 15:3-8

> For I delivered to you as of first importance what I also received, that Christ died for our sins according to the Scriptures, and that He was buried, and that He was raised on the third day according to the Scriptures, and that He appeared to Cephas, then to the twelve. After that He appeared to more than five hundred brethren at one time, most of whom remain until now, but some have fallen asleep; then He appeared to James, then to all the apostles; and last of all, as to one untimely born, He appeared to me also.

First, we see he appeared to quite a few people. At one point, he even appeared to 500 people at once. If over 500 people came up to you declaring they saw a particular popular band live at a concert, would you not believe that there must have been a concert you had not heard about? It only stands to reason that if so many people make a claim and testify to being eye witnesses to this claim, it probably happened. Why then did so many people still disbelieve? Why do we still disbelieve?

1 Corinthians 15:12-19

> Now if Christ is preached, that He has been raised from the dead, how do some among you say that there is no resurrection of the dead? But if there is no resurrection of the dead, not even Christ has been raised; and if Christ has not been raised, then our preaching is vain, your faith also is vain. Moreover we are even found to be false witnesses of God, because we testified against God that He raised Christ, whom He did not raise, if in fact the dead are not raised. For if the dead are not raised, not even Christ has been raised; and if Christ has not been raised, your faith is worthless; you are still in

> your sins. Then those also who have fallen asleep in Christ have perished. If we have hoped in Christ in this life only, we are of all men most to be pitied.

Even with all the eye witness accounts, many still refused to believe it and thought it was crazy talk. Paul, going with their reasoning, tells us that if this is true, we are all to be pitied as we have been teaching a false god and some had even died for this false god and were cut off for all of eternity. Thankfully, it does not end there. He continues in verse 20 with:

1 Corinthians 15:20

> But now Christ has been raised from the dead, the first fruits of those who are asleep.

Paul says Christ is the first fruits. The first fruits of a harvest was a sample brought to the priest as an offering to the Lord. The farmer was not allowed to harvest the rest of his crops until after this offering had been made. In the same way, there was no resurrection until the first fruits had been brought forth. Christ is the first fruits. He alone made it possible to be raised unto eternal life with the Father. Many people teach of Christ. They say all you have to believe is that he was the son of God. The movie The Passion of the Christ portrayed the death of Jesus. Catholics wear a crucifix around their neck as a reminder of what he did for them on the cross. This is all fine and dandy but alone, it amounts to nothing. Without the resurrection, there is no salvation. This is why an empty cross is a more accurate symbol and is actually the one used by Protestants. As my old pastor used to say, a hole in the wall to represent an empty tomb would be the most accurate of all. Christ is no longer on the cross. He is no longer in the grave. As important as his death is, his resurrection is even more so.

Matthew 27:50-53

> And Jesus cried out again with a loud voice, and yielded up His spirit. And behold, the veil of the temple was torn in two from top to bottom; and the earth shook and the rocks were split. The tombs were opened, and many bodies of the saints who had fallen asleep were raised; and coming out of the tombs after His resurrection they entered the holy city and appeared to many.

    This is something I missed for the longest time. Although I had read Matthew countless times, I never really noticed it although it is a huge event. The dead came out of their graves and went into the holy city. Imagine seeing your dead relatives come up to you one evening to talk. You look around and see your neighbors are being visited by their dead relatives as well. It is absolutely amazing. I have no idea how I never really saw this in Scripture. How could I skip this part in my brain? While it may look like all this happened upon the death of Christ, we need to carefully look at the text. It speaks of the death of Christ, moves into people rising, and then goes back to speak about the death. This almost appears contradictory to the teaching of Christ being the first fruits. How could they rise before Christ? The thing to pay attention to is in verse 53. It says, "and coming out of the tombs **after** His resurrection they entered the holy city and appeared to many." Christ raised himself and appeared to many. In the meantime, there were others who had previously died and were now walking into the holy city. Talk about amazing! One other thing to notice is the fact that all who had previously been resurrected died again at some point. They were brought back to life in an earthly sense but this was temporary. At some point, they would die again. They had surely been resurrected but not in the same sense as Christ. He was now in a glorified and eternal state that we will all one day see.

1 Corinthians 15:22 & 51-53

> For as in Adam all die, so also in Christ all will be made alive......Behold, I tell you a mystery; we will not all sleep, but we will all be changed, in a moment, in the twinkling of an eye, at the last

> trumpet; for the trumpet will sound, and the dead will be raised imperishable, and we will be changed. For this perishable must put on the imperishable, and this mortal must put on immortality.

We can see there will be a literal changing of the body upon the resurrection. It calls our physical body perishable and mortal whereas our next body will be imperishable and immortal.

Philippians 3:21

> who will transform the body of our humble state into conformity with the body of His glory, by the exertion of the power that He has even to subject all things to Himself.

John 20:26

> After eight days His disciples were again inside, and Thomas with them. Jesus came, the doors having been shut, and stood in their midst and said, "Peace be with you."

The doors being shut refers to them being locked. Jesus had just been crucified and the disciples feared they would be next. They were frightened and in hiding so they locked their doors. Nevertheless, Jesus appeared in their midst. There are some out there that teach our glorified body will be able to pass through walls since Jesus somehow appeared inside a locked house. I do not necessarily subscribe to this theory as it is not what the text says. It simply says he stood in their midst.

Luke 24:31

> Then their eyes were opened and they recognized Him; and He vanished from their sight.

While I can't confidently teach that Jesus could pass through walls, I can say he could do something even greater. First, it alludes to the fact that he could hide his appearance and make himself appear differently to people. Second, it says he vanished from their sight. I think a better interpretation of his standing in their midst despite a locked door is that he just appeared. Just as he could vanish, he could reappear somewhere else. He did not have to pass through a wall. He just appeared where he wanted to be.

Philippians 3:21

> who will transform the body of our humble state into conformity with the body of His glory, by the exertion of the power that He has even to subject all things to Himself.

According to Philippians 3:21, we will all have this same glorified body upon our resurrection.

Not only do we have a physical resurrection and change to look forward to someday, we also have a spiritual resurrection. The difference is that one happens the moment you become a believer in Christ and receive the gift of saving faith while the other will take place at a later time.

2 Corinthians 5:17

> Therefore if anyone is in Christ, he is a new creature; the old things passed away; behold, new things have come.

Romans 6:4

> Therefore we have been buried with Him through baptism into death, so that as Christ was raised from the dead through the glory of the Father, so we too might walk in newness of life.

Titus 3:5

> He saved us, not on the basis of deeds which we have done in

> righteousness, but according to His mercy, by the **washing of regeneration and renewing by the Holy Spirit**,

Before Christ, we were spiritually dead. After Christ, we have a newness of life. We become regenerated and renewed. A band called Decyfer Down has a great chorus that speaks of dying to oneself and living in Christ:

Decyfer Down

> I am so alive, since you took my life
> I'm walking dead now, only you remain
> I take the life you gave, I walk from the grave
> I'm walking dead now, I am not afraid![i]

It is not speaking of a physical death but rather a spiritual one. We must die to ourselves and be raised in Christ. This is the symbolism represented at baptism. We go under as if we are being laid in a grave upon death. We come up cleansed as if being resurrected in the new life of Christ. Baptism is a representation of what occurs at the moment of salvation. The day will come when we will experience this in the physical as well but it is only because Christ did it first to make it all possible.

1 Corinthians 15 closes out with encouragement:

1 Corinthians 15:57-58

> but thanks be to God, who gives us the victory through our Lord Jesus Christ. Therefore, my beloved brethren, be steadfast, immovable, always abounding in the work of the Lord, knowing that your toil is not in vain in the Lord.

While we are all on this Earth trying to live our lives, Jesus came to this Earth to die for our lives. This is the real reason for the season. Presents and family time are fun and can even be an important time of togetherness but we should never let it overshadow why it is we even have a season to celebrate. It is because of this one baby boy born under the most peculiar of circumstances so that we might one day have eternal life through Him. I urge you all to ponder this thought the next time you celebrate Christmas. In fact, I issue another challenge to you. I urge you to ponder this thought at every waking moment of your Christian life for without it, we would not have life at all. We've already won and we have something great to look forward to, so stand fast in all you do and trust in the Lord.

---

[i] Decypher Down, Walking Dead (from album: End of Grey) [Sony, 2006]

17 CHOOSE RESPONSIBLY

How often have you pondered the doctrine of God's sovereignty? Anybody who has ever given it even the slightest amount of thought will realize it is not an easy subject to digest. Where does sovereignty end and free will begin? If God is truly sovereign, is He also at fault? These are some of the questions we are going to address in this chapter. In particular, we are going to go over man's role in regards to the sovereignty of God. While being countless takes on the matter that vary is subtle ways, there are 3 basic positions on the subject.

1) If man has free will, God cannot truly be sovereign

2) If God is sovereign, man cannot be held accountable for his actions as he has no free will

3) God is sovereign yet man is still accountable for his actions

I cling to the third option. By the end of this chapter, it is my hope that you, the reader, will as well. Before we get into man, we must begin with God. We know God is sovereign because the Scriptures tell us so. Before we go into the Scriptural backing, let's define sovereign. Dictionary.com defines sovereign as "having supreme rank, power, or authority."

Psalm 103:19

> The LORD has established His throne in the heavens,
>   And His sovereignty rules over all.

Ephesians 1:11

> also we have obtained an inheritance, having been predestined according to His purpose who works all things after the counsel of His will,

Job 42:2

> I know that You can do all things,
>   And that no purpose of Yours can be thwarted.

2 Chronicles 20:6

> and he said, "O LORD, the God of our fathers, are You not God in the heavens? And are You not ruler over all the kingdoms of the nations? Power and might are in Your hand so that no one can stand against You.

We can clearly see that God is in control at all times. All things work after the counsel of His will according to His purpose and His purpose can never be thwarted. This sovereignty flows into all areas. Nothing escapes it. Psalm 103:19 said His sovereignty rules over all.

Proverbs 16:33

> The lot is cast into the lap,
>   But its every decision is from the LORD.

Matthew 10:29

> Are not two sparrows sold for a cent? And yet not one of them will

> fall to the ground apart from your Father.

Psalm 135:6-7

> Whatever the LORD pleases, He does,
>   In heaven and in earth, in the seas and in all deeps.
> He causes the vapors to ascend from the ends of the earth;
>   Who makes lightnings for the rain,
>   Who brings forth the wind from His treasuries.

Galatians 1:15-16a

> But when God, who had set me apart even from my mother's womb and called me through His grace, was pleased to reveal His Son in me so that I might preach Him among the Gentiles

Most people don't take issue with the teaching of God's sovereignty so long as it is spoken of in these terms. Up until now, all the verses have been describing God and leaving man out of the picture. Man naturally likes to live a guilt free life. Nobody likes a buzz kill. It is unfortunate that, even in the Church, God is viewed as sovereign so long He does not interfere with our own free will. This concept is unbiblical. Not only does heaven and earth fall under the sovereignty of God but so do we as people. The Lord rules over all things; even mankind.

Arminianism, as well as many other theological views, portrays sovereignty in a much different light. While admitting that God has absolute control over His Creation, they make the claim that He created mankind with the ability to make free choices not influenced by any outside source. In other words, the effect is not the result of a cause. It is totally free in a libertarian sense. While it is easy to reconcile our own desire for control with this view, it simply is not what we are told in Scripture. Everything in this world is the way it is because God created it to be so. As we have read, His plans can never be thwarted. I have to agree with John Piper on this one.

John Piper

> It is not merely that God has the power and right to govern all things but that He does so always and without exception.[i]

God's sovereignty was not a one-time thing that ceased upon the end of Creation. It is a continuing force that never fails, never runs out, and never steps aside. God's sovereignty is not merely the *ability* to govern all things but actually *IS* the governing of all things.

Acts 2:23

> this Man, delivered over by the predetermined plan and foreknowledge of God, you nailed to a cross by the hands of godless men and put Him to death.

Even the crucifixion was ordained by God. Notice what is taking place in the verse above. It says that godless men will put him to death. Godless men will nail him to a cross. Both of these things imply man will make the choice to perform a wicked act. However, take note that it only takes place because of the predetermined plan of God. It also speaks of His foreknowledge. Do not be confused. God didn't ordain His plan based on choices He knew man would make. Rather, He knew the choices man would make because He foreordained it to be so.

Acts 4:27-28

> For truly in this city there were gathered together against Your holy servant Jesus, whom You anointed, both Herod and Pontius Pilate, along with the Gentiles and the peoples of Israel, to do whatever **Your hand and Your purpose predestined to occur**.

This just drives home the previous point. Both Herod and Pontius Pilate had gathered together to go against Christ. In fact, they were not alone. It says the Gentiles and people of Israel had gathered as well.

There were countless people rising up against Christ. This was of their own doing and their own choices. They had made the decision to put Jesus to death for his claims. Again, however, notice that it says they were only doing whatever God's hand and purpose had predestined to occur. While they were making their own choices in life, there was only one way it would play out. God had decreed it to be so and that was the end of it.

Another example in Scripture of God's sovereignty mixing with man's choices is in the story of Joseph.

Genesis 37:18-22

> When they saw him from a distance and before he came close to them, they plotted against him to put him to death. They said to one another, "Here comes this dreamer!" Now then, come and let us kill him and throw him into one of the pits; and we will say, 'A wild beast devoured him.' Then let us see what will become of his dreams!" But Reuben heard this and rescued him out of their hands and said, "Let us not take his life." Reuben further said to them, "Shed no blood. Throw him into this pit that is in the wilderness, but do not lay hands on him"--that he might rescue him out of their hands, to restore him to his father.

This entire discussion is between Joseph's brothers. Their discussion is not being coerced or pushed in any direction. It is not being moderated. They are freely coming up with a plan to murder Joseph. At the same time, Reuben takes it upon himself to talk them into sparing his life and throwing him into a dry ditch instead. It is quite the intricate plan from the minds of depraved individuals. On the surface, it appears they are free to do as they wished with nothing else to lean on other than their own desires. While it is true that they were coming up with this plan on their own, there is more to the story.

Genesis 50:20

> As for you, you meant evil against me, but God meant it for good in order to bring about this present result, to preserve many people alive.

Joseph was rescued, sold into slavery, and eventually took on a prestigious position under the pharaoh. None of this was by accident. Scripture is clear that God had a plan and that plan was good.

Romans 8:28

> And we know that God causes all things to work together for good to those who love God, to those who are called according to His purpose.

While Joseph's brothers were free in the choices they made and the actions they took, they only made these choices because God had decreed it to be so. God is always in charge. Sometimes he actively takes part in an event such as the destruction of Sodom and Gomorrah whereas most times, He allows man to freely make decisions and choices. However, even when left to freely make decisions, they are always within the constraints of God's sovereign plan and purpose.

As I said earlier, most people do not take issue with God's sovereignty so long as it leaves man out of the picture. It is my hope that, by now, you will see even man does not escape God's sovereignty. You may even be nodding to yourself in agreement. However, what if I were to add man's salvation to the equation? Would all heads cease movement in the vertical sense and start turning side to side instead?

A.W. Pink, The Sovereignty of God

> To argue that God is "trying His best" to save all mankind, but that the vast majority of men will not let Him save them, is to imply that

the will of the Creator is impotent, and that the will of the creature is omnipotent.[ii]

Acts 13:48b

and as many as had been appointed to eternal life believed.

While I firmly believe salvation falls under the sovereign decrees of God, I do not intend on getting into a breakdown on God's Election again in this chapter as it was covered in full in chapter 6. While it is true that only those whom God has called unto Himself will respond to the call of Christ, I want to focus on those whom He **does not** call unto Himself. Are these men condemned because of God? Should they be given a free pass? Can they possibly be guilty if they were never given a fair chance or opportunity? No, no, and yes!

While they are indeed condemned, it is certainly not because of God. These men will never choose Christ because God has ordained that they will not but this does not mean God is responsible. Each man is still held accountable for his actions as we saw earlier in the cases of the crucifixion as well as Joseph. There is no free pass to be given because each man is guilty to begin with. The term used to describe man's responsibility despite God's sovereignty is *compatibilism*. The two are not mutually exclusive as many would state but, rather, complement each other quite nicely.

Ezekiel 18:20

The person who sins will die The son will not bear the punishment for the father's iniquity, nor will the father bear the punishment for the son's iniquity; the righteousness of the righteous will be upon himself, and the wickedness of the wicked will be upon himself.

Matthew 12:37

For by your words you will be justified, and by your words you will

> be condemned.

John 9:41

> Jesus said to them, "If you were blind, you would have no sin; but since you say, 'We see,' your sin remains.

James 1:13

> Let no one say when he is tempted, "I am being tempted by God"; for God cannot be tempted by evil, and He Himself does not tempt anyone.

We can see a clear distinction being taught between God's sovereignty and man's responsibility. While there is no doubt that God is sovereign and all things only come to pass because He ordained it to be so, it is equally as true that man makes his own choices without being forced or coerced. His choice will always be the outcome that God decreed but man will gladly make it. This is because man is bound by his nature and that nature is wretched and fallen.

Genesis 8:21b

> for the intent of **man's heart is evil** from his youth;

Jeremiah 17:9

> The **heart is more deceitful** than all else
>
> And is desperately sick;
>
> Who can understand it?

John 3:19

> This is the judgment, that the Light has come into the world, and men loved the darkness rather than the Light, for **their deeds were evil**.

John 3:20a

> For everyone who does evil **hates the Light**

We simply follow our nature. Before salvation, Romans tells us we were slaves to sin. We had no choice but to give our all to it. However, this was not a grudging state or grueling task as we did it with pleasure. Our hearts were evil. Our hearts were deceitful. Our deeds were evil and we hated the Light. We hid from the Light lest our evil deeds should be exposed (John 3:20). Our natural inclination was to sin. We were in bondage to sin but we enjoyed every minute of it. This is why we are still found guilty for our sins despite following God's sovereignly decreed plan.

Romans 6:22-23a

> But now having been freed from sin and enslaved to God, you derive your benefit, resulting in sanctification, and the outcome, eternal life. For the wages of sin is death,

While once enslaved to sin, we are now enslaved to God. The unregenerate man, despite being in full accord with God's sovereign decrees, is still found guilty and deserves death. He works as a slave to sin and, as a result, he will be paid death for wages. It is what we all deserved as we have all sinned and fallen short of the glory of God (Romans 3:23). Thankfully, God chose us and called us unto Himself. This does not make us perfect but it does make us His own. When we sin, we are covered by the blood of Christ.

Romans 5:9

> Much more then, having now been justified by His blood, we shall be saved from the wrath of God through Him.

Romans 8:30

> and these whom He predestined, He also called; and these whom He called, He also justified; and these whom He justified, He also glorified.

We still sin daily in our battle with the flesh but we will not see Hell for it. We have been justified by the blood of Christ. His blood alone has fully atoned for our sins. There is no more debt. The blood was substitutionary.

Romans 6:1-2

> What shall we say then? Are we to continue in sin so that grace may increase? May it never be! How shall we who died to sin still live in it?

Just because we are covered by the blood does not mean we are to abuse our justification. Paul makes it very clear that we are not to sin so that the grace we fall under may increase. We are free from sinning. This is where we differ from the unregenerate man. We have a new nature in Christ whereas he does not.

Do you love God? If your answer was yes, do you feel as if you were forced to say so? Just as we love God and desire to serve Him with all we have so does the unregenerate man hate God and desires to hide from the Light. Even if an unsaved individual says he is not at war with anyone, his refusal to submit to the authority of God proves otherwise. A man cannot serve two masters (Matthew 6:24). He is either for God or he is against God (Matthew 12:30). Both sides serve their masters willingly yet both sides do so only because God has declared and ordained it to be so. God is sovereign yet we are responsible.

John Calvin, Bondage and Liberation of the Will

> ...we allow that man has choice and that it is self-determined, so that if he does anything evil, it should be imputed to him and to his own voluntary choosing. We do away with coercion and force, because this contradicts the nature of the will and cannot coexist with it. We deny that choice is free, because through man's innate wickedness it is of necessity driven to what is evil and cannot seek anything but evil. And from this it is possible to deduce what a great difference there is between necessity and coercion. For we do not say that man is dragged unwillingly into sinning, but that because his will is corrupt he is held captive under the yoke of sin and therefore of necessity will in an evil way. For where there is bondage, there is necessity. But it makes a great difference whether the bondage is voluntary or coerced. We locate the necessity to sin precisely in corruption of the will, from which follows that it is self-determined.[iii]

---

[i] John Piper, http://www.monergism.com/directory/link_category/Sovereignty-of-God/

[ii] A.W. Pink, The Sovereignty of God [Bridge-Logos, 2008], pg 3

[iii] John Calvin, The Bondage and Liberation of the Will [Baker Academic, 2002], pg 69-70

ABOUT THE AUTHOR

Travis W. Rogers is a diligent student of the Word and has served in the U.S. Navy since 2000. For the past 4 years, he has acted as Protestant Lay Leader onboard the USS Benfold (DDG-65) and led others in their spiritual walk in the absence of a Chaplain. It has been his deepest desire to see others come to the knowledge of truth and experience a deeper walk with God.

Travis and his wife, Tiffany, are blessed to have a son and two daughters.

Made in the USA
Lexington, KY
12 December 2011